Mary's Diary

MARILYN FRIESEN

To order additional copies of this book, contact:
Bookwhip
1-855-339-3589
https://www.bookwhip.com

There is something so beautiful, sweet and inspiring about Mary, the mother of Jesus. I can't seem to wrap my mind around the thought; she was only thirteen or fourteen when she had Baby Jesus. Just imagine how meek and humble she must have been, otherwise God wouldn't have chosen her! I feel like I've 'gotten close to Mary, *(Mary'am)* while writing this "diary" and I hope you, the reader, can learn to appreciate her beautiful qualities also. Some of us don't believe in worshiping saints, but it sure wouldn't hurt to learn from her example.

My Baby, mine?
Nay, all Heaven
Claimed
that Child divine.
My heart ached so
For scriptures
Warned
Of pain and woe.
...The years rolled
On
And people
Thronged
From early dawn...
But some showed
Hate
Oh, Jesus flee
Before too late!
My faith is shaken
The Son of God
By soldiers taken.
Too pained to cry.
He suffered so
Before He died.
Oh, glory, glory
My Son arose,
So ends my story.

CALENDAR

Tishri
September/ October
Marchesvan
October/ November
Kislev
November/ December
Tevet
December/ January
Shevat
January/ February
Adar
February/ March
Nisan
March/ April
Iyyar
April/ May
Sivan
May/ June
Tammuz
June/ July
Av
July/ August
Elul
August/ September

4097

4097

9th Nisan

March 20th

Dear Diary,

I will always be grateful to my dignified, elderly
Uncle Zachariah for teaching me to read and write that
long ago summer when I was ten. There are some thoughts
that are too personal, too profound to give voice to but they must be
shared and writing is the best way.

In all sincerity, Mary'am

(That's my Aramaic name)

10th Nisan

March 21st

DEAR DIARY,

How can I get close to *HaShem*? That is what I am striving for. *HaShem* means The Name, and is the most respectful title I know to call The Holy One. We hesitate to speak His name out loud, but I pray He will pardon me if I write it from time to time. There is something about *Adonai*, hallowed be His name that is dreadful, but I long to have a more meaningful relationship with Him.

This week I have been thinking much about the sacred prophecies concerning the *Mashiach. (Messiah)* What kind of woman would *Yahweh* choose as the mother for His Son? It would be such a delightful honor and a privilege, I wish it could be me.

Did you hear my tiny sigh? I suppose hundreds, nay, thousands of *talitha* (girls) more honorable than I have longed to cherish the Holy Child as their own, but they were not chosen, so why would I be chosen to bear Him?

We are of the lowliest of the lowly. The Judeans, particularly the religious leaders, look down their long noses at us Galileans. Do they not think we are so dim-witted about understanding the finer points of the law?

The Anointed One's mother would be someone without the many faults that I have! I imagine she will be someone like the virtuous woman our noble King Solomon described many years ago. She would diligently reach out to the poor, the needy, and in her tongue would be the law of kindness. I have a lot to learn in that area.

I am guessing that the Mother of the *Mashiach*-- what elegant
sounding words--would need to be someone of royal birth so she
would know how to groom her Son to become the future King.
But, I am of the right lineage! David is my ancestor.
We have the precious documents right here in our chest to
prove it. They have been passed down from generation to
generation and are among our most valuable possessions.
Yea, I must admit though that thousands of others
are of the same lineage.
This one last time, I will confess it hurts deeply that I will not be
able to mother *HaShem's* Son. He must be born of a virgin,
I am soon to be married.
You will not ere in your thinking, no? I am joyfully
planning to wed my beloved *Yosef,*
But when I do, this dream will have to die forever. It is most
difficult to lie down. It has been a secret desire for so long, but
I will, I will show a brave face and cheerfully walk hand in
hand with my betrothed for all my days
and if perchance some other *aant'at* (woman) gets this blessing
during my lifetime, I will try to be happy for her.
Perhaps it will be my own daughter!

DEAR DIARY,

My thoughts have been soaring heavenward with a yearning to be one with *HaShem*, especially today because the sky has shone like molten gold. The air seemed to be hushed as if it is standing on tiptoe in the *Shekinah* of *Adonai,* (the glorious presence of the Lord of Lords.) Many furlongs away, the Sea of Galilee is rippling under this same glorious sunset. If it reminds me so much of Paradise here, what must it look like over the waves?

I was lingering near our almond tree, which is shrouded
with a thousand pink and white flowers.
Over my arm hung a basket filled with herbs, since I had
just finished gathering them from our dew-scented garden
when a dazzling dove swept by, catching my attention.
She was such a bright contrast to the beautiful horizon. As
I gazed upon her, I wondered if, perchance, this would be
the time I would see where her little fledglings were hidden.
I have been watching her closely for some time now.
I was also enjoying the fresh, invigorating breeze against my cheeks.
It was sweetly scented with the fragrance of a million early flowers.
Then a voice seemed to float towards me.
I do not know how else to describe it. I looked
around but saw no one. There was such a
quietness, calmness in the twilight stillness;
I was not afraid, just mildly curious. While my eyes swept the
glowing sky and dewy green landscape, a marvelous being appeared.
He seemed to materialize out of thin air, but for some reason I was
pleasantly intrigued rather than terrified. Then in angelic tones, this
glorious creature, whose raiment dazzled like snow, spoke to me.
"Hail, you are highly favored; the Lord is with
you; you are blessed among woman."

I had been gazing rapturously upon him but these
words made me feel uneasy so I lowered my eyes.
How could someone such as I be highly favored?
Surely my thoughts had become too lofty and *El' Shaddai* was
about to rebuke me.
He knows how deeply I have longed to mother His Son.
Perhaps that was rash and foolish for a *talitha* such as I.

"Fear not Mary'am," he said gently, "for you
have found favor with El Shaddai!"
My hand pressed against my throat, "Me?" I managed to gasp.
He nodded, his whole being glowed with a
radiance that could only be described as celestial.
Although certain that I was in the presence of one of the angels of *El'
Shaddai,* for some reason I felt serene, more composed than I have ever
felt before. It was almost like I had been lifted to a hallowed plane.
The cares and burdens of life had fallen away, as if I had shed them
for a time, like waterfowl sheds water. After a momentous pause,
he continued.
"Listen! You will conceive and birth a Son and call Him *Yeshua.*
He shall be great and be called the Son of the Highest. The Lord
God shall give unto Him the throne of His father, David.
He shall reign over the house of *Yaakov* forever;
of His kingdom, there will be no end."
"Excuse me," I raised my eyes to shyly meet his gaze, "But how
can this be, since I am a virgin and know not a man?"
"The Holy Ghost shall come upon you, the power of the
Highest shall overshadow you. Therefore also that holy thing
that shall be born of you shall be called the Son of *Adonai.*

A trembling shook my body at these majestic words; I think my face
must have gone ashen. It was more than I could comprehend. Carry
the Son of God! That was my heart's desire! Something I had longed
for more intensely even than to be married to my *chavivi,* (beloved).

My knees felt weak. Surely something so holy and
glorious could not be happening to such an insignificant
handmaiden of the Lord. I must be dreaming!
The serenely glowing face of the angel came back into focus
once again, when he spoke it was in a gentle, soothing voice,
about things that were at least a little more ordinary.
"I have more good news for you. Your relative, Elisheva
(Elizabeth), is carrying a son in her old age; this is her
sixth month, she who was called infertile."
I gazed at him in awe, open-mouthed and speechless. Elisheva is my
favorite aunt. How wonderful! How very, very wonderful! Won't Imma
(Mama) be delighted when she finds out. She always felt so sorry for
her eldest sister because she never knew the joys of motherhood.
He beamed, "With El Adonai, nothing shall be impossible."
I sank to my knees and with clasped hands, replied in a hushed voice,
"Behold, the *talitha* of the Lord, be it unto me according to your word."
While I watched wonderingly, the angel's feet rose from the
ground, his magnificent wings spread out, I saw him gradually
rise higher and higher until he flew from my sight.

After he was gone, an invisible but very hallowed sense of *Shekinah*
surrounded me. Never have I had such profound love, such
happiness and complete tranquility permeate my being as it did at
that moment. It must have been a foretaste of the joy of Paradise.
As the sensation faded, I am certain that *HaShem*' touched me
in a very profound, personal way. I cannot express what He has
done for and to me. When He left I quietly murmured…
"Alleluia El ohim Yisrael!"

Shortly after this experience, the evening sun set and the
sky grew dark quickly. The night air was laden with the
perfume of roses, the sky was brilliant with stars.
With so many stars, it seemed like there was surely
symbolic messages of great portent written in the sky,
messages that only the learned could read.

I slipped into the house for this little scroll, my reed pen and a small clay lamp. I am now sitting on a large flat rock near our lovely almond tree trying to write with the aid of the stars and the lamp's flickering glow.

"Holy, holy, holy," I breathed, loath to leave this sacred place, yet knowing the hour was growing late.

I seemed to have been wrapped in an aura of other— worldliness for the rest of the evening.

When I wandered back into the house, Imma was busy chopping up vegetables for a stew. Soon the aroma of simmering onions permeated the air.

My sister, Hana, came in from milking the goats. She handed me the milk, which I absentmindedly strained through cheesecloth into another container.

The hum of voices ebbed and flowed around me, but I hardly noticed. *Abba,* (father) came in, after washing up, he said the *Banoah* (blessing). After he was finished eating, the rest of us gathered around the table.

"You are quiet tonight," Imma observed. Her voice barely penetrated my thoughts.

"Mary'am." Abba's hand was poised above the scroll he was reaching for. I looked up when he spoke my name. "Your mother just spoke to you."

"I'm sorry, Imma, dear. Did you want something?"

"How quiet you are since coming in."

My cheeks felt like they were growing warm, so I looked down, and dipped a sop into the common bowl.

"I'm feeling--thoughtful, tonight."

Abba and Imma exchanged a quizzical look, but I didn't feel like I could explain anything, not yet.

It is hard for me to grasp the magnitude of what actually happened just a few short hours ago, harder perhaps because everything else in my small world continues in just the same down-to-earth way it always has.

I hope people can comprehend that it is not that I am so special. It is what *HaShem* is going to do through me. I am just His poor earthen vessel.

29th Nisan

April 9th

DEAR DIARY,

With tears in my eyes, I must admit this has been a low time for me. The feeling I had, as though I was dwelling in heavenly places, has faded to a rather forlorn memory, and I am not well. After scattering a few kernels of corn to our flock of chickens,
I crept behind the goat-shed to be sick. It did not relieve the queasiness in my stomach very much.
A number of days have passed since the Shining One paid me a visit and I am feeling so very ill. I thought I had been able to conceal my queasiness fairly well, but Imma has noticed me as I pick at my food.

Knowing my mother the way I do, I am not at all surprised that she was concerned. She shooed the little ones, Dorcas and Naomi, off to play, and sent Hana on an errand.
We had the heart-to-heart talk I yearned for. She is just the kind of mother who takes to heart anything that affects the lives of her loved ones and she wants to help them.

At first, Imma was amazed when I told her I was with child by *HaShem.* Nay, astounded would be more the correct word. As I unfolded the narrative and she plied me with questions, her amazement turned to delight, then to holy wonder.

"Oh Mary'am, Mary'am," she breathed, "how is it that *Adonai, hallowed be His Name,* has considered our family worthy of such a high honor?" I think she marveled more than anything at the fact that I had seen an angel, at first. Then she questioned me much about what the Heavenly Being looked like. After that she grew quiet and thoughtful as the reality of my condition began to sink in.

"The Mother of the *Mashiach*," she murmured in a hushed voice. "Your father and I have discussed it, and in our longing, we hoped it would come in our generation. But to choose us! How can it be that *Yahweh* would choose us, and Navara (*Nazareth*) is such an unworthy town,"—she gestured with her hands, and shrugged, saying,

"With high taxation plaguing our community, so many have stopped trying to an honest living; they have taken up banditry in order to put a morsel of food in their little ones' mouths.

"Yet you are a virgin, even as *HaShem* commanded!"

She fell silent and straightened the tassels on the *tefilah* (prayer shawl) she was embroidering with the Star of David. When she looked up and met my gaze, I saw that her gentle brown eyes were troubled.

"Mary'am, we haven't considered the implications...."
My heart was pounding, Imma slipped her warm hand into
mine. We were both silent. I am grateful that she would
never imply that I might have been unfaithful to Yosef.
Our bond is too close and sweet for such suspicions to arise. Besides,
she knew, as I do, that the *Mashiach* is supposed to be born of a virgin.
Yosef is too HaShem-conscious to rush things, and has carefully
refrained from even kissing me, lest his passions be unduly aroused.
But sadly, others will not look upon it the way we do.
Even dear, kind Abba would have reason to be concerned.
He knows the strength of a man's desires far more than I,
in my innocence, could ever imagine. He may even think
I had been overtaken along some shadowed lane!
That is impossible, of course, because my Abba and Imma have
never allowed their daughters to be out alone after dark.
I am confident that I*mma* will have a tactful way
of bringing the glad tidings to Abba.
It may take him awhile to come around, but he has always
been an understanding father, so surely he will believe me.

Please, please let it be .

30th Nisan

April 10th

DEAR DIARY,

It's eventide once again, the room is growing dim.
The future looks bleak. How will I survive if Yosef
puts me aside, and chooses another?
How can I face the stares and the snide remarks of my
friends? Perhaps my own father will forbid me to live at
home if Yosef convinces him I have been unfaithful.
The law requires that a woman caught in adultery be
chased away, with stones hurled at her until she dies.
But no, surely Yosef, my, *chavivi,* would never go to that extreme.
His heart may be broken, but he loves me. I know he does!

My thoughts are getting carried away.
It is *Yahweh's,* Son that I am carrying. He will surely take care of
His own. Yea, it is *Yahweh's* son, but the mother is so human.
El' Shaddai, I will try my best to trust in You no matter
what comes. I must fight these anxious thoughts.
Oh, Holy One, forgive me for being so worried and dispirited. Your
precious Son deserves someone more courageous and sweet than
I to nurture Him in the coming months and years, but since You
deemed me worthy, I promise to do my best, nay, my very best.

DEAR DIARY,

Today was cloudy and dark; a gloomy sort of day.
Not even my companions, whom I regularly meet at the
well, were in the mood to linger and chat for long.
I guess it is because there is a chill in the air.
The clouds are dark and lowering.
Quite likely by nightfall the early rains will have begun in earnest.
It sure feels like a day for huddling in our mud brick homes,
as close as possible to the little fire in the brazier.
I wonder how my long-time friends will treat me once
they can tell that I am carrying a *tinoki*, little child.
Will they give me the look that so many reserve for
aant'at, women of ill repute? I shiver to think of it.
I can imagine Shoshoni making hurtful remarks to
Tamara, but what about Abigail and Rebecca?
Will they continue to treat me kindly?
When I was just a wee thing, I asked my Imma why she
had called me Mary'am because someone taunted me
that it meant a bitter sea, or something like that.
I can remember so clearly how she responded.
She immediately dropped what she was doing and reached out
her arms to me. I snuggled on her lap while she tucked the
end of her stole around my body. This is what she said:

"Oh, Mary'am, where did you hear that? It also means 'longed for one.' You were such a tiny baby, so sweet and perfect. I wanted to find a name that would suit such a lovely *tinoki*. Then I thought of the Mary'am in the *Torah*, (the word of *El Shaddai*), sister to Aharon and Moshe. *(Aaron and Moses)* Do you remember the story?"
I nodded vigorously, happy that I could tell my Imma I knew which story she meant.
"When I saw your tiny face," she continued, " I wondered if *Adonai* would have something special for you to do, like He had for that other Mary'am and it just seemed like the right name."
She gave me an affectionate squeeze and a kiss on my forehead and I scampered off to play.
I have never forgotten what she said.

DEAR DIARY,

I am getting a little rounder every day. Only I can tell, but soon the
secret will be out.
While I write this, Hana is sleepily getting dressed; when
she is ready, we need to fill the water jugs at the well.
While mothers are waiting to fill their vessels,
I often gather the restless little ones around me for a story. It is such fun!
Will they, who used to be so friendly, snatch their
children away from me after I show?
Will they treat me as if I am unclean, as if I have leprosy?
Will I ever again hear Hadassah or Damaris lisp
in their trilling voices,
"Mary'am, Mary'am, tell us a story. Tell us a
story. You are the best story teller!"
Isaiah and Titus used to run up also and we would
sit in the shade of the old sycamore tree.
Even the clusters of *aant'at,* hushed their
banter sometimes, although I can tell that some pretended not to listen.
I really love telling the story of Ruth, of course it does not
appeal to the boys. I am so glad she is part of my lineage!

Ruth said to her mother-in-law, "Whither thou goest,
I will go, whither thou lodgest, I will lodge, thy people
shall be my people, and thy God, my God."

What beautiful, timeless words they are.
If Yosef decides to marry me, I would like to say those
words to him as part of our marriage ceremony.
I wonder how Ruth would have felt if she was carrying the
secret I am carrying. My, I would love to talk with her;
I think she would be so understanding.
My communion with *HaShem,* hallowed be His Name, was special this
morning. Somehow it doesn't really matter so much anymore how others
respond to me since I felt that glorious sense of *Shekinah*, His presence.

DEAR DIARY,

Imma shared my precious secret with Abba. I wonder if she has ever kept a secret from him for so long before, but I guess she was afraid it would trouble the waters.

He, in turn, has talked to my future in-laws. Their reaction was not good. Yosef's stern preoccupied air and his father, Yaakov's condemnation have driven me to tears.

Yosef's mother, Hilde, is a heavy-set woman,
with iron gray hair.
At one time, I thought she had such an affable personality,
but when we met on market day, in front of the fig
and date stall, she was as cross as two sticks.
She glared at me and snatched at Imma's sleeve to
propel her away so that they could talk together.
What was I to do? Where was I to look?
I kept my eyes averted until the stain of embarrassment receded
from my cheeks. The multitude jostled me about indifferently
and I timidly caressed my slightly rounded abdomen.
*Oh baby, baby, I wish I could protect you from the cruel
stares, the snide remarks of an unkind world!*

Eventually, I found myself beneath the baker's awning, but even
that delightful aroma did nothing to soothe my distressed spirits.
"A honey cake for you, Mary'am? You look like you
need a little something sweet to cheer you?. One
with date sauce drizzled on top, perhaps?"
I had walked on before even realizing it was to me the
baker was calling. I looked back then, and saw the look of
compassionate concern on his face. I hardly know him, but he
cared about me, a young *talitha,* from the same synagogue.
Thank you, Yahweh.

　　　Marilyn Friesen

I continued to trudge down the dusty street, past the heaps of fruit in their sprawling baskets, past the mat and basket weavers stall. When I came to the booth where stacks of pottery were displayed, I stopped.
I hardly noticed when a donkey, heavily laden with
copper pots and pans, clattered to a stop beside me.
The owner noisily began to unload his wares.
With arms folded as if in self- protection, I stared off
into the empty space just beyond the village,
then slowly turned around and trudged down the other
side of the street. I did not know what to do
since Imma was carrying the basket.
Eventually, Imma located me.
When I saw the tenderness in her troubled yet
compassionate look, my throat filled with emotion.

Hilde broke away from my mother and strode off.
Disapproval stuck out from her like seams on a garment
worn inside out. Imma took me by the elbow
and gently lead me away from the crowds.
"We will return home, yes? Hanalei can make our purchases."

It seemed to take us a long time to make our way through the
hot, irritable market-goers but the crowds eventually thinned,
as we trudged down the narrow winding
path into our own neighborhood.

I slumped on our front stoop and buried my head in
my arms, while Imma went to search for Abba.
Hanalei came over and sat down beside me,
but I did not care to talk.
She gently laid her hand on my leg; we leaned
into each other without saying anything.
Abba's deep voice instructed Hana to attend to the shopping.
She gracefully arose, the thought crossed my mind about how
tall and slender she was, just like our aunt, Elisheva.

I am small, with softly rounded curves, like Imma.
We both have large, dark eyes, perhaps we both looked
troubled at this time. I was left alone to face my father,
but Imma hovered in the background.
"Mary'am, look at me."
My gaze lifted upwards but it was hard to keep it steady;
his face was so stern. He took a long breath and expelled
it slowly before crossing his arms in front of him.
"Come, we must have a talk."

The petals of the almond tree showered around me
when I brushed against them. I could not allow myself
to think about the memories they stirred up.

Abba leaned against the inside wall of the barn as I stood
beside our goat, apprehensively stroking the smooth snow-
white hair on her nose. Imma was once again
hovering somewhere behind her husband, my father.
"Daughter, are you thinking clearly?"
I uttered a little gasp, wondering what he could be getting at.
It seemed to take so long before he continued talking.
"Your Mother and I have known for a long time how deeply you
love *El' Shaddai, hallowed be His Name,,* and we appreciate it."
He paused, Imma stepped forward to rest her hand on his arm.
"I believe you would long to be the Mother of the *Mashiach,*
but do you realize how impossible that would be?
Your longing has turned into a flight of the imagination
which is making your betroth's family very disturbed."

"Oh, but, Abba! It is true!" He held up his hand to silence me.
"I know you believe it is true and your Mother has told
me why it seems possible or even probable to you."
He reached out and took Imma's hand into his own brawny one.
"I am sorry, daughter, but the *great Mashiach* would not
come to the likes of us who are of lowly birth."

Marilyn Friesen

My whole body sagged and his look softened.
"He will be a King, *yeled.*
We do not think less of you for having such hopes and
aspirations. Your mother and I refuse to believe Hilde's
suspicions that you have been unfaithful to her son."
My head sank and my face burned.
"I suspect you may be overwrought with all
the excitement of your engagement."
I started to tremble; Abba does not usually speak to
me in such a serious, almost stern manner.

"Your mother has a relative whom we have not visited for a long
time. Her name is Elisheva. Do you remember her? She
resides at *Ain Karim,* near *Yerushalayim (Jerusalem),*
with her aging husband who is a priest."
I nodded. Of course I remembered Elisheva. The angel had
shared some very special news about her that I had told Imma,
but I had not been brave enough to share it with Abba.
Elisheva is such a lovely lady, so elegant, so gracious.
I had stayed at their home for several weeks after Passover the year
I was ten. I had tried to imitate her for a long time afterwards.

It was her tall, stooped, gray-bearded husband who had taught me
how to read and write. I probably shouldn't admit who taught me.
Some of the religious authorities think it is better to burn
the Holy Writ than for a woman to learn to read it.
Oh well, this is private. I'm not planning to share it with the world.
"Your Mother and I have decided that it might be best
if you would visit them until all this excitement calms down."
I came back to the present with a start.

"Me? Alone? Oh Abba, how could I?" I wailed and flung
my arms around him. He gently rubbed my back.

"What you have been saying has been causing too much of a stir,
daughter. We do not want the—the unthinkable to happen."

I leaned back to get a good look into his eyes. "The
what?" A *divorce*. "Oh." My head sagged against his
rough, homespun tunic. *Or maybe even stoning.*
"Yosef agrees to wait until you come back to make a decision."

I do not think I heard much more of what he had to say even while
my head reeled with the enormity of the decision; my heart sank
like a stone. *They are sending me away.* Abba *does not believe I am
carrying the Christ Child; else he would not be doing this to me.*

I am to go to a far-away place. Is it not a five days journey?
Why, that is like traveling to the ends of the world. Must I go alone?
I will be so lonely—and frightened!
I will need to sleep in the wilderness among strangers, night
after night. What if they are aloof, or even unfriendly?
What if burglars attack? Haven't there been
more sightings of lions recently?

When I started to sob brokenly,
Abba awkwardly turned me over to my mother.
I was dimly aware as he mumbled something about getting back
to the shop but I was crying too hard to pay much attention.
It seems like everything is going wrong in my life.
Everything has been turned upside down.
I have been feeling so nauseated, blue much of the time, and on top
of that I will be bundled off to live with near strangers—in disgrace!

I am sure it is Hilde's doing. That must be what
she was scheming with Imma about.
Will my beloved Yosef come to see me before I must depart?
Oh, I hope so! Dare I even call Yosef my beloved anymore?
It is a relief that he does not lash out angrily at me,
but I am anguished by his extreme shock, horror and disappointment.

I had been so thrilled at the thought of becoming the mother to the Son of *HaShem*, hallowed be His Name, but that was because I didn't foresee the future.

Oh, *El Shaddai, hallowed be Thy Precious Name,* please forgive me for thinking such wicked thoughts. I long to be the saintly woman the Anointed One deserves for a mother. But I'm not. Oh, I simply am not.

The pain of Yosef's disappointment is crushing me. Oh Yosef, Yosef, Yosef, do you not realize I would never intentionally hurt you? I am so numb with grief at the thought of losing you that I can hardly function.

Oh dear, this is such a long writing, and I blotched it with my tears!

14th Sivan

May 23rd

DEAR DIARY,

Yosef has not greeted me warmly for many days. I might as well say it like it really is; we haven't even exchanged more than two words. He is polite, but I have seen him treat strangers with more cordiality than he has bestowed on me! I feel ill with despair.

Marilyn Friesen

15th Sivan

May 24th

DEAR DIARY,

Somehow, something must have been said at home, my younger sisters don't treat me so sweetly anymore. Dorcas and Naomi give me troubled looks as if they cannot quite understand what has changed with me. They are not as spontaneous with their hugs as in former days. Am I just imagining this?

Hanalei and I used to be as close as burrs in sheep's wool but now she is somewhat reserved in my presence.

Imma had thought she was old enough to share in our secret, but from the way she is acting, we wonder.
Perhaps Hana is concerned about how her friends will react when they find out her older sister is expecting a *riba*, (child), and before the wedding.
Perhaps she is afraid this will lessen her own chances of finding a nice, respectable husband. She had been telling me how much she admires *Caleb bar-Reuven* for some time now.

Dear old Abba has been quiet and unsmiling since our discussion. I wonder so often what he is really thinking. I wish he would not council with *Yaakov* so much since Yosef's father is so perturbed with me. Now that Abba is so distant, Imma waits until he is out of the house to show her loving sympathy. It is then that the tears, the soothing healing tears, flow freely and we can talk. Naturally, Imma does not feel ill as I do, so she is still quite optimistic about it all. I know she does not consider my story a fantasy, like Abba, Yosef and his family do though.

What would I do without my Imma to lean on, to comfort
me? Imma is touched that a daughter of hers would be
considered worthy to be the mother of the son of *Adonai,*
our Almighty God, but is deeply concerned that Yosef
is considering having divorce papers written out.
Isn't it strange that two such conflicting emotions
can dwell in the same heart?
Being thrilled yet at the same time deeply concerned
seem so opposite from each other.
Imma feels for me; I am glad she is praying
that things will work out somehow.
We have whispered together
about how dreadful it would be to be identified
as an unwed mother.
I do not believe *Yosef* would ever have me stoned,
but would not the stony disapproval of our
community be almost harder to bear?

I know that every day I am growing a little rounder,
someday the sacred secret will be revealed.
But unfortunately, or is it fortunately,
I will be far away by then, for *Abba* insists that
I must go, for who knows how long.

2nd Tammuz

June 10th

DEAR DIARY,

The caravan driver escorted me to Zechariah's door. The trip was long and tiresome, but not as dreadful as I feared. I so often felt the Lord's Shekinah so close.

Zechariah's stone house is situated in a serenely beautiful valley.
It is a spacious dwelling with many archways and pillars.
It even has marble floors. That is such a contrast to our
own dirt floor. Oh, well, I love our little home just as much,
if not more, because that's where my family dwells.

I was so enthralled with the cooling fountain in their courtyard
and all the exotic flowers and plants surrounding it. It was such a
refreshing change after trudging through the wilderness for so long.

It is very strange to have a room all to myself, such a soft, high bed!
Yet, I will miss having my sisters snuggling down close beside me.
What a blessing it was to be enfolded in Elisheva's
warm embrace! She seemed so happy to see me.
It was like feeling an unexpectedly warm and
balmy breeze in frigid weather.
We had such a meaningful visit right after I arrived that I did not
even remember how exhausted I had been feeling 'til much later.
To my amazement, she knew immediately
that I was carrying *Yahweh's* son.
The baby leaped within her, and then, do you know
what?—Elisheva started to prophecy like the patriarchs
of old. I have never heard anyone do that before!

It thrilled me right to my toes when she said, nay, almost shouted,

"Mary'am, you are very blessed among women!
The baby you are carrying is very blessed indeed.
How can I be so fortunate that the
mother of our Lord would come and visit me?
As soon as you called out, the babe knew who you were
and leaped within me."
What a shiver of awe ran down my back.

She told me I would be blessed for believing.
Can you imagine the comfort I felt after the
despondent atmosphere at home?
She also reminded me that all that the angel told me would come true.
Perhaps, if *Abba* could have heard her faith and
enthusiastic response to my pregnancy,
he would have believed also.

It filled me with such a deep joy to know
that Jehovah has regarded my low estate. His quiet, unassuming *talitha*,
I clasped my hands in wonder, as I thought about His Holy Name.
Future generations will call me
Banoah, (blessed) and indeed they are surely right.
Hundreds, perhaps thousands, of *aant'at* would
gladly trade places with me.
The Mighty One has done marvelous things, holy is His name!
Somehow I sense that when He reigns, He will not only show mercy
to those of our generation that fear him, but will extend mercy for
generations to come. I cannot comprehend it. It is so amazing!
Under His guidance, I just know that wrongs will be righted.
Those that we call powerful will be of no more value
than the poor in spirit; the hungry will be satisfied,
but the rich will go away empty in spirit.
How can I know these things?
I simply don't know. It does seem like a spirit of
prophecy has descended upon me also.
I am eagerly waiting to see what it means.

As you may well know, my despondency has been
lifted, carried away on wings of joy!

I just know these are going to be pleasant,
meaningful months,
helping Elisheva. I am really looking forward to it.
Surely, we will have many inspirational visits.
I really need them to help me to grow into the role
Adonai ordained for me.
Verily, *HaShem* knew what was best when I was sent here,
even though I had been so distressed about it.

3rd Elul

August 9th

Dear Diary,

Amen, *Alleluia El' Elohim!* I am home again,
and the best news of all, Yosef is willing to take me as his wife.
Yes, you read correctly. *Yosef is willing to take me as his wife!*
I will not be put aside after all. I will not have to endure
the shame, the awful humiliation of a divorce.

I clung to him as if I would never let go while the tears
rained down my cheeks. He kept caressing my face,
wiping at the tears with his thumbs, saying,
"There, there, everything's alright."

I wasn't the only one that was crying though.
He turned aside more than once and used his sleeve to
dry off his wet cheeks. He confessed that he was
also relieved that it had worked out this way. This tells me
a lot about how devoted he is to me, and to *HaShem.*
After we got over our joyous reunion, we sat down on a stone
bench in a shady nook and he told me what caused him
to change his mind. It was a dream. How thrilling!
The Lord God, *Yahweh,* sent an angel to visit Yosef during
the night in order to convince him to marry me after all.

Don't tell anyone, but it makes me nervous to think
HaShem is so closely involved in our lives.

And, oh, by the way, Hilde is being more considerate
towards me now that Yosef made his decision,
after he told her about the dream. Perhaps she cannot quite
believe it, but if her precious Yosef is happy with me,
that is good enough for her.
Whatever he does seems to be almost perfect in Hilde's eyes.
I wonder if I will ever act that way towards my sons.

Yaakov, on the other hand . . . (Sigh) . . . Why is he so
critical of me? He is the one that had agreed that Yosef
marry me in the first place, now he is so opposed.
Maybe it would be better not to talk about him.
It makes me too distressed.
It is enough that Hilde is more approachable.
Yosef, my *chavivi,* Yosef, is just wonderful!
In fact, I wonder if having that dream has made him
even more tender-hearted and kinder than before.
(If that is possible!)
Taudi HaShem

11ᵗʰ Elul

August 17ᵗʰ

DEAR DIARY,

I will confess to shedding some tears tonight because we will not be having a traditional, Jewish wedding. Such a ceremony would be inappropriate in my condition.

Lo, I had dreamed for years about what my *chuppah* would look like and I was hoping it would be a tall graceful canopy of fine white linen. My parent's friends from *Bethashbea* make the best. Perhaps they would have even given us a good cut in price.

I was hoping to have the most fragrant pink roses that we could find tucked in here and there on the canopy. I'm sure, Rizpah, another dear friend of my mother's, would have gladly given us some for the occasion. She grows the loveliest damask roses, nicer than those of anyone I know. Ever since I had first admired Yosef, as a wee *talitha* of seven spring times, I have often dreamt of him, with me standing beneath our wedding canopy.

Imma has some vines clinging to the front of our white brick house. I was hoping to plant some into pots well ahead of time, to have them bordering the archway on either side of the canopy, interlaced throughout the roses. Would that not have been ever so lovely?

My dearest friends and I have often chattered about how delightful it would be to help each other prepare for our *mitzvahs.*(ritual immersion symbolic of spiritual cleansing). I can almost feel the nervous excitement I would have experienced as they helped me into my wedding garments.

They would have taken turns
brushing out my wavy hip-length hair and
we would have chattered excitedly
as they busied themselves preparing all the rest.

I love to imagine the look of awe on Yosef's face when
he sees my hair uncovered for the first time.

It is fortunate, Imma that, you cannot see my woebegone expression.
I must, so I will refrain from pining over the loss of a
beautiful wedding when I have the more glorious honor
of nurturing the son of *Adonai.*

To think that I am the one woman in the whole wide world
to have been given this responsibility, this honour!
And yet I dare not think that He made a
mistake because I am so unclean!

What a joy it is to be accepted into Yosef's favor once again.
I could collapse with relief

4098

25 Elul

August 31st

DEAR DIARY,

According to tradition, this was the first day of **Cre**ation. Because of our great history of storytellers that pass our heritage from one generation to the next, it is easy to believe.

Yosef is not quite finished building our cottage. He thought it would be better if we had a quiet wedding and finalized the *ketubah*, (contract) before a rabbi, even if it is not a year since our betrothal. I already know he will continue to treat me as if we are only engaged.

We hope that will stop tongues from wagging. People have been gossiping about me dashing off to Zachariah's home so soon after we were betrothed. I can tell that some have noticed that I am, well, chubbier than I, uh, ought to be before the wedding.

It was such fun helping Yosef plaster mud on to the
entwining bamboo that makes up the roof.
I looked more like a mud-splattered little *tinoki*
than a ladylike bride that day.
It was a joy to help them scatter the straw that went up
between the layers of mud, but he would not even consider
letting me haul up any of the straw or mud.

Marilyn Friesen

He must think I am quite fragile. I sure don't feel delicate anymore. I am so thankful that we now have the privacy of our own little house; it is really private now that the roof is on, and thoroughly dried.

It is just so pleasant to be with him all the time.

Our house is pretty sparse, right now, but who cares. Yosef comes from a long line of joiners and is an excellent carpenter. I'm sure he will make some wonderful pieces of furniture once he finds the time.

DEAR DIARY,

There is something so special about being married
on the same day that Chava, was presented to *Haddam*,
on the last day of creation.

Our wedding week was delightful.
I'm glad Yosef took the time off from work to be with me and visit
relatives, even though we didn't have a lovely, formal wedding.
Those seven days were sweet, however,
Yosef feels he must treat me with restrained dignity because the
baby I am carrying is not his, but belongs to the Holy One.

We went for long walks over the surrounding hills and
meandered through the marketplace from time to time.
It was so pleasant, just the two of us walking hand in hand.
It truly feels like our hearts are knitting together as one.

I wouldn't have ever dreamed a man could be so
gentle, so understanding, so devoted!
Marriage seems to bring out the best in us. Apparently, we both
want so badly to say only kind and tender things to each other.
I feel incredibly secure in his presence,
I look forward to sharing the rest of my life with him. I am
most confident that he will make an ideal human father for
our little boy and that's why *EL Elohim* chose him.
Why am I wasting time writing in a mere diary? I haven't seen him
since our noon meal, I am lonesome already. I wonder if he can
find something I can help him with?

Love Mary'am

Cheshvan 2nd

October 18th

DEAR DIARY,

Look how the weeks have flown, I have not written in my "dear old diary" for over a month. Actually, I do not have time now because Yosef will soon be ready to go for a moonlit stroll down by a delightful stream that only flows during the rainy seasons. It is something we haven't had time for in a long time. I will have to be careful because I am great with child and certainly I mustn't slip. Of course with Yosef's arm around my waist, I need not fear.

Cheshvan 7th

October 23rd

DEAR DIARY,

We have heard such startling news. Everyone of King David's line will
have to trudge off to Beth Lechem to be taxed.

That includes Yosef and me, since we are both descendants of David,
one of us through Solomon, the other by a more obscure son, Nathan.

I wonder how that will work with my pregnancy;
I am so near my birthing time?

It feels like every city in the whole country will be
getting mixed up like a big pot of mixed lentils or beans, with
everyone traveling hither and yon to reach the city of their origins.

What an unsettling time for our baby to be born. But I
know His Heavenly Father is watching over us. He knows
exactly what is going on in His frail children's' lives.

Cheshvan 9th

October 25th

DEAR DIARY,

Something sad has happened.
In an effort to understand it better, I will try to see it
from my beloved *Mimi's* (grandma's) point of view.

Sevta (my grandmother) sang a happy little tune
about Adonai's love while she briskly wielded a hoe
in her tiny garden patch behind the house.

It was a fresh spring morning, my, did she ever enjoy working
among her thriving plants. It seems like every day there were
new things to marvel at, such as a sweet new bud kissed
by a dew drop on her rosebush or quietly watching
a mother bird as she scurried about feeding her adorable,
but always frantically hungry young.

Sevta smiled as she stooped to scratch out more weeds from her
row, how like her own clamouring children so many years ago.
She looked up when a donkey brayed and a feeling of
dizziness swirled around her. She leaned on the hoe,
waiting for the feeling to pass but it only got worse...

*What is happening to me? Maybe if I can get to the
house and rest awhile, I will soon feel better.*

Darkness overshadowed her. She could not see where she was going.

If I can only make it to my bed, I'll be okay.
Let me take a drink of water... She reached out her hand,
groping for direction. She took one step, then another.
The hoe clattered to the ground beneath her weakened hand.
I must not fall, I must not. Mary'am will be stopping
in shortly like she always does on her way to market,
I don't want her to find me on the ground.
She is with Child. I must not frighten her.
Seven more steps and you'll be at the door.
You can do it, Rebecca, you can do it. You can see a little bit.
Keep going, just keep going.
"Oh, *Adonai,* help me," she probably cried, as she fell
against the doorframe and tumbled to the ground.

But no human heard her.

I'll lay down my pen with a sigh, but soon I must write some more.

Sundown

DEAR DIARY,

This is the eventide of the same day. I'm still writing
in a detached sort of manner. It must be because of the sad,
almost melancholic mood I am in.
Mary'am rested her hand protectively
on her rounded abdomen as she gazed apprehensively to
the top of her father-in-law's mud brick house.
Yosef was up there somewhere, hard at work mending
the roof before the latter rains descended.
She wanted to talk to him.
She tested her weight on the first rung of the ladder,
And then stepped higher, and higher.
Soon her brown eyes were peering over the top of the balustrade.
Yosef straightened when he saw her, his own eyes
widened. "Mary'am," he exclaimed, "be careful!"

"I am," she responded, trying to keep the tremor from
her voice. "I wanted to ask you something."

He nodded, looking ready to leap to her assistance
if she so much as blinked an eye.

"Since we are in such a hurry to get to Beth Lechem,
I was wondering if I should put off visiting
Mimi (grandma) 'til another day."
"Do whatever you think is best, darling,
but please get off the ladder!"

Mary'am hummed a happy tune as she scurried off
to market with her basket slung over her arm.

She took the shortcut, bypassing Sevta's house
entirely since Mimi lived closer to her folks
than to where she had been receiving council from her husband.

But her conscience wouldn't leave her alone.

She will be so happy to see you!

But I go nearly every day. She'll understand if I miss just this once!
It's urgent that we leave for Beth Lechem as soon as possible.

But what if she needs me?

Needs me? Sevta? She's the most lively, energetic Mimi I have ever seen!

But what if, what if...

I'll stop in on the way back with some fresh fruit. Sevta is so
thrifty, I'm sure she doesn't splurge on any very often.
Why not go now? It's not that far out of the way.

With a self-depreciating smile, for impulsively changing her
mind, Mary'am headed towards her grandmother's house.

What is that strange lump huddling next to Sevta's doorstep? Is it
a dog? No, it's too colourful to be a dog. A beggar perhaps? I do
wish the beggars would take pity on an elderly widowed woman
and go elsewhere. But she is too merciful to shoo them away.

Mary'am hurried closer. "Mimi!" *Oh, I am so*
glad I listened to that quiet voice.

Soon, my precious grandmother will be cared
for by gentle efficient hands.

19th Chisleu

December 3rd

DEAR DIARY,

Because of one delay after another, we were not able to go to the city of David to be taxed as soon as we had planned. Tragically, my *Mimi,* (grandma), went to be with her fathers.

She was so dear to me. I couldn't bear to leave her when she was so low, but she passed away, so we will depart after the funeral.

This will be all for now, for I want to take one last look at her calm, still face before we follow the bier to the grave site.

DEAR DIARY,

I am not feeling very brave today even though the stars are twinkling
brightly in the otherwise black, early morning sky. Yosef is
loading Balaam, our donkey.

Somewhere, far, far away, in a place called Beth Lechem,
the stars are also shining, I suppose, but the track is
so rough and dark between here and there.

There are treacherous mountains just a few furlongs
from the road we must take, who know what kinds of
animals might come prowling around at night.

It will take us many days to get there,
this is happening so close to when the baby is expected to
arrive! I have never been far from home, except for the time
I went to see Aunt Elisheva. I dread this journey.

At least this time I will have Yosef with me.
What a consolation. My deepest fear is for the Baby,
because I am so near the end. Oh, if only it would have
worked out to have left earlier. Will He be alright?

I know we will not be traveling alone but
that is not much of a consolation.

Cousin Abigail, once my dearest friend, will be in the company,
but she has been cool and aloof since my condition was revealed.
It might be easier to handle than the scathing remarks Shoshoni made to
Tamara at the marketplace. I think she knew I might have overheard her.

My sister, Hanalei, claims Shoshoni has always been jealous
of me, but why, I am not that special. Some have called me
sweet and pretty but she is beautiful and sophisticated. Besides,
her father is a prosperous merchant and we are so poor.

It has been such a trial since the villagers shunned
me While whispering behind their hands.

I am so lonely for the merry prattle we *aant'ats* used
to share when we met at the well each morning. Now
everyone just falls silent or walks slowly away while
my eyes dolefully follow them. Oh well, it could be so much worse.

For some reason, and I am not sure why,
it has not made that great of a difference that Yosef married me.
Is it because of *Yaakov*? I probably shouldn't have written that,
yet I do know that someone is spreading rumors that *Yosef*
is not the father of my child. Obviously, I am too far along
for it to have happened since we were betrothed...

They have been saying that I had been overtaken by a Roman
soldier. They do ravage careless maidens at will, especially while in a
drunken stupor. Of course, that is so impossible! My parents would
never let their daughters be alone if they had to be out at night.

My *aleichem*, (neighbors), could be making cutting
remarks to my face but most of them don't.

I mentioned Shoshoni, but really,
most of them don't say anything much . . . in my presence,
at least. Sometimes I fear that the Little One I care about so
deeply may have to suffer much worse persecution than I.
Oh, how I yearn to protect Him!

Why do such thoughts come to me? Most people are confident that the *Mashiach* will be a glorious King and will rule with a scepter of gold. If that is the whole truth, why would a poor *talitha* like me be asked to be His mother? It is confusing. I am so inadequate for such a privilege, and it is such an awesome responsibility.

I wish Imma could come along to Beth Lechem. It would be such a comfort. But, on the other hand, maybe it is better that she is not able. She tends to worry so, saying things like,

"Be sure to keep warm, do not let yourself get too tired."

She has told me that countless times, or so it seems.
How can I keep from getting tired?
I am worn out already, and we have not even begun. Imma is scurrying towards me with a nicely wrapped parcel of food for the journey. I really must go assist her.

DEAR DIARY,

Traveling has not been so bad after all. I didn't realize how beautiful much
of this country is. The olive gardens and fields are such a bright green
at this time of year. I can always anticipate a splendid view
over the next hill, which makes all the climbing worth it.
We have traveled one day's journey, we stopped a little while ago.
I think the monotonous plodding of the donkey relaxes me. I
suppose if I was not used to riding donkey, I would be more
stiff and sore, but that is our main means of travel.

All around us little campfires are brightening up the
evening scene. Yosef also has a cheery fire going.
He is so caring. He will hardly let me do anything, which is
why I am writing in my journal while he bustles around,
much to the hilarity of fellow travelers. He seems to think he
needs to protect me as though I am a delicate flower.

He has the wonderful potage that Imma sent along,
it's simmering over the fire; soon I will be munching
on some of her good homemade bread.
For special times, she makes it the way that Ezekiel
recommended and I love it so much.
It has millet, lentils, and spelt in it, besides barley and wheat. It makes
me homesick for her and our memories of forming loaves together.

Abba was sadly unapproachable, he turned stiffly away
when I wanted to give him a goodbye hug.
Oh, if only he would believe that something so pure and
holy has actually happened to his little *tinoki*.
The angels visit so long ago was wonderful. I wish I could
renew that feeling of
blessedness more often. It would give me more courage.

P.S. The potage was warm and nourishing; it will be our last hot meal
on this trip. From now on, we will be dipping into our leather bags of
cheese curds, dehydrated fruits and so on. Our goat skin water will
have to be sipped sparingly because of the route we are travelling.

I am exhausted so I must quit. I feel like I could sleep well
anywhere tonight, even on a folded blanket under the stars.

DEAR DIARY,

Abigail edged over to me this evening while her husband was involved
in a heated discussion about politics with some of the other men. She
clasped my hand and confided that she was certain I was carrying the
Christ Child and had been afraid to tell me earlier. I was consoled, but
I still had to fight the temptation not to be hurt since she had not stood
by me earlier, if she truly believed. I hope she will be my dear friend
once again when we return to Navara.

As she turned to walk away, I saw that her thickly fringed eyes
were sad in her small, pale, face and I couldn't hold it against
her for shunning me. Would I have done any better if rumors
had been spread about her while she was betrothed?

Yosef is heading my way now. I am sure my peace-loving husband
wearies of all the angry critics of the Romans. While the sun was
setting, Yosef and I had an inspiring conversation about the coming
of the *Mashiach,* and our great *El' Shaddai, hallowed be His Name.*

Yosef is such a deep thinker, he studies the Torah, and
the prophets so diligently. I am able to ask him many
questions. His answers are so beneficial to me.

After a while, we started singing a Psalm. It starts like this:
*Oh El' Elohim how excellent is your name in all the
earth! Who has set your glory above the heavens?*
A little later it mentions considering the heavens, the work of His
fingers, and the moon, and the stars which He has made.
Yosef told me that the stars are foretelling the Christ Child's
birth, but that is too much for me to comprehend.

It is a beautiful starry night, and our hearts are lifted up in praise
to the great *El' Shaddai, hallowed be His Name!* Some of the other
pilgrims joined us in singing. It was *Banoah,*(blessed) indeed.
People are friendlier now that we are on the road. *Alleluia El ohim Yisrael!*

I had better roll up my little scroll and carefully tuck it
back into its leather case for it is time to sleep.

Good night, Imma, *dear.)*

22ⁿᵈ Chisleu

December 6ᵗʰ

DEAR DIARY,

First light, if you can call it that, I heard a wind come up during the night and by morning the clouds had blotted out the sun. The *Geshem,* (latter rains) descended upon us with a vengeance, we were miserable even before Balaam's saddlebags were properly repacked. Yosef and I donned our thick woolen cloaks,
but it was impossible for me to hang on to the donkey's reins without rain trickling up my sleeves. That was so uncomfortable.

We slogged along silently, going uphill most of the way, or so it seemed. I noticed that our fellow travelers were not calling out to each other so exuberantly anymore. The clouds still look thick and dark the closer we get to our destination.

DEAR DIARY,

Our Matriarch, *Rachael*, wife of *Yaakov*, passed away this season of the year.
I surely hope it wasn't as miserable a day as this.
It is already the middle of the day, not that you can tell by
looking at the sky, we have stopped for a short break.
Poor Balaam's head is hanging down;
he looks pathetic. The rain is streaming in rivulets
down his shaggy mane and back.

Care for some soggy flatbread?
I think I'll stick with dried fruit for this repast.
I'm already looking forward to nightfall so we can huddle
back under the shelter of our goat skin tents once more.
I know that there won't be any campfires tonight. The others
are moving around, preparing to start traveling again,
so I must tuck this parchment in the safest, driest place I can think
of, inside the folds of my belt under my heavy woolen cloak.

I am so chilled. Hope I don't get the sniffles. Abigail is quite ill
with fever. It is such a miserable time for her to have to travel.

24th Chisleu

December 9th

DEAR DIARY,

Yes, there had been more rain today,
but I am not complaining because it eased off
towards late afternoon.
Just as the red and gold of sunset covered the sky,
I saw a very distinct rainbow. What an exceedingly
rare glorious sight! My heart lifted up to *El' Elyon* in
praise and gratitude for His wondrous works.
What made it even more of a blessing is that since
Shabbat started at sunset today, we were able to rest,
worship and fellowship without getting soaked.

DEAR DIARY,

This has been a very, very hard day.
I am almost too weary to write
but I must because such memorable things are happening.
My body is being wracked with pain.
I've clung to the poor donkey's neck and let my veil conceal my
face so Yosef would not see how difficult it has been for me.
Not that I fooled him for one moment.
He is so distressed, he keeps asking whether or not we
should press on to reach Beth Lechem's *khan,* (inn), by
nightfall or if he should let me rest more often.
As it is, many have tramped on ahead.
We are left behind with the roving wild animals, the *geshem,* and
perhaps even bandits for company. But I do not need to think of that.
My emotions are fragile for many reasons, somehow, I still know
that *Adonai, hallowed be His Name,* will care for us and
His own beloved Son.

DEAR DIARY,

This page will surely be unreadable
because I can't keep the tears from falling. We finally reached Beth
Lechem by nightfall but there was no room at the *khan, no* room at all!
All the rooms above the shelter for the animals were overcrowded
with wealthy wayfarers, much wealthier than us.
In the courtyard below, the animals had scarcely
enough room to shuffle around.
The innkeeper seemed apologetic, but helpless.
Yosef pleaded for him to suggest someplace—
anywhere for us to stay, but the poor, overwrought
innkeeper shook his head sorrowfully.
"I am sorry. So sorry," the innkeeper said,
stroking his long, kinky beard agitatedly. He lifted his
hand to point at the people crowding around.
"See this multitude? They too are in the same
predicament that you are in."
"But is there not somewhere, anywhere that we can go?"

In Yosef"'s desperation, he reached out to clutch
the steward's striped garment.
"Look, it is not for me that I am concerned,"
Yosef continued, "t is for my wife! She is young,
slight of build, yet great with child.
I fear that all this traveling may bring travail
upon her earlier than it ought. We need to
find a shelter where she can rest."
The paunchy innkeeper's brow furrowed as he gazed around,
as if looking for direction.
Someone plucked at his sleeve, demanding attention,
with a scowl he nudged him aside.

"On yonder ridge is the town, but you will fare no better
there. Nary a house is not overfilled with guests at this
time. Many have long awaited the census already, and I fear
no one is willing or able to take in more travellers."
"But is there no where for us to go? We are of the lineage of David!"
"'The lineage of David?
Aye, that should help, should help. Know you not of any relative you
could stay with?"
Yosef wrung his hands. "I know of none. We
should have inquired earlier."
The innkeeper stepped back and fumbled with his sash.
"This small town is not able to contain all those of
David's line." He admitted, sighing heavily.
"Yonder ridge has its share of caves. Many of them will be used
as stables in this present predicament, but if you can find
a little rest in one of them, you are welcome to it. I
will send a servant after you with fresh straw.
"If you require a midwife before the night is over, I may find a moment
to check into it, but it will be nigh impossible to secure one at this time.
More than one woman is in the same dire condition as your sweet wife."
In gratitude, Yosef took his hand, clasped it, then reached for the lead
strap on the donkey so we could clamber awkwardly down among
the rocks in search of a grotto turned into a stable. I lowered the veil
back over my face, lest Yosef would see the despair written there.
We did find a cave, however, without too much searching.

When Yosef was able to get the clay lamp lit, it seemed more cozy
and inviting. It was rather crowded, unfortunately. *Yosef* is trying to
persuade some of our fellow cave dwellers to take their lowing,
smelly, burden bearers and hustle off to give us a measure of peace.

I am so weary that all I want to do is remove my wet garments,
find something dry to wear, and try to rest. Yosef was rather
anxiously fluffing up the fresh straw, which was delivered by a
young lad with a hand cart, he is now shaking out our blanket.
I laid the baby's swaddling strips near the fire to dry.
Fortunately, we had kept one blanket well packed so it wouldn't
get wet on the trip. It was somewhat damp in a couple places
but it was better than nothing. We sat beside a central fire
until I was warmed up, which seemed to take forever,
then we crawled under our one rather thin blanket together.
In the stall next to ours are two donkeys, tied up,
their owners are lounging against a nearby wall.
At the far end of the cave, there is some activity going on.
I think a shepherd is about to aid a ewe giving birth.
Will there be two male 'lambs' born before the night is o'er?

DEAR DIARY,

I feel that my time is drawing nigh, I am anxious. It is frightening to think of having my baby without my mother, or a midwife nearby. I am worried about the baby. What will happen if He comes before we can move on to a better dwelling? This cave is not clean enough!

Two of the wayfarers, a middle-aged couple, were cooperative and helped us out. Some of the others growled that they were here first and were not at all inclined to be agreeable under such chilly weather conditions.

I fear they have been indulging too long in the wine that is red.

Oh, surely, surely *Adonai, hallowed be His Name,* will be with me during this difficult time. My every breath is a prayer that *Adonai* will protect His own Beloved Son and me.

By the dejected slope of *Yosef*'s shoulders, I can sense that he feels that he has somehow failed me and us. I must stop writing now and tell him how warm and inviting it all looks by the light of the lamp. Surely these stabbing pains will ease now that I have a place to rest. It seems too soon for the little one to make His appearance.

FESTIVAL OF LIGHTS

25th Chisleu

December 9th

<u>Chanukahs</u>

Dear Diary,

He's come! *Yehoshua* has come!
I cannot begin to express my gratitude and adoration.
What a privilege it is to be the first one to
hold the treasured Son of Yahweh.
Oh dear, tears are running down my face again. He is so precious.
I just can't say it enough.
It tugs at my heart strings when I see how incredibly
tiny and helpless He, the Son of *El'Shaddai,* is.

I wanted to cradle Him longer, much longer,
but Yosef yearned to hold Him also.
Yosef is sitting in the straw nearby and it makes me rejoice to see
the man I adore cuddling the most wonderful Baby in the world.

DEAR DIARY,

This has been a strange and wonderful night.
Yosef and I had no desire to sleep so we leaned against each other,
gazing adoringly at the wide-eyed baby in our arms.
I half wished that Yeshua (how quickly we have shortened His name)
would cry so I could cuddle and hush him gently with a lullaby or two.
But He was so wide awake and calm, looking
at us with those beautiful eyes of His.
I almost think He knows who we are;
but do not all fond parents imagine their babies are
smarter than they are capable of being?
Who knows, maybe this one is. It will be interesting and
delightful raising such a sweet boy. If I ever have another one,
it will be much too easy to compare him with Yeshua, I fear.

It has been so cozy, almost homey in the cave tonight. A wee,
sweet-faced kid scampered over to us and stared at our tiny
boy inquisitively. When our baby made a soft mewing sound,
the baby goat looked so surprised that I started to giggle.

Earlier, we heard some brawlers carrying on.
They made me feel most uncomfortable, but someone must have
told them to either be quiet or leave so those of us who wished to
sleep could sleep. There are others sharing our crowded quarters
but they are far enough away that
we are afforded some privacy. It is so calm and peaceful now, as a
little halo of light from the lantern surrounds our little family.

Hark! I hear something faintly in the distance! It's music, like singing, or chanting perhaps. It must be the loveliest melodic sounds this world has ever heard. What can it mean?

26th Chisleu

December 11th

DEAR DIARY,

Yosef rushed to the entrance to see what is happening.
I stayed where I was to protect our dear child from a draft, but oh
what a rich, vibrant choir of voices I hear out there somewhere.
It sounds so heavenly! Why doesn't everyone else wake up? It is
glorious, so glorious. Is that a tiny smile on my wee one's face?
Maybe He knows what it is all about.
Oh, HaShem, what have I gotten into?

Yosef came back with some strangers.
I was surprised to see that they were shepherds.
I had been expecting to see angels!

I would love to tell you all about the exciting visit that we had with
the shepherds, but truly I am over-tired and must close for now.
I need to get some sleep because we have been awake all night.

2nd Tevet

December 15th

DEAR DIARY,

I am so sorry, Imma dear, I still have not written about
the shepherds' visit.

We had to gather our bundles and find a more suitable place,
rather than that damp chilly cave. Yosef was most anxious to find
a proper home for our little one; we were able to rent an attractive
one-room dwelling in a cluster of other similar houses.

I am not sure how we will pay the rent but Yosef feels we ought
not to return to Navara until the infant is stronger, of course he is
right. It is quite likely he will be able to find work as a carpenter's
helper for the time being. They seem to be always in demand.

I have been both amazed and exhausted by all the
company that has been streaming through our door.
It seems like everyone knows someone in this shepherd
town who is related to the shepherds on the hills.
They have been crowding in, groups of twos and threes,
even more, for the last several days because they want to hear about
the wondrous angelic visit for themselves and see the little *tinoki*.

Some go away disappointed. I heard one woman say, "He looks so
ordinary. I thought his face would be glowing or something."

I'm sure another one thought I was out of earshot when she
remarked about the patches on the elbows of Yosef's robe.

"Surely, nothing spectacular could happen to such poor people," she said. "Why, they are just like us."

It is a consolation that her friend said, "Didn't you see how neatly they were patched? I'm glad to know they are ordinary people. If He is the *Mashiach,* maybe He will have more understanding for the common folk.

3rd Tevet

December 16th

DEAR DIARY,

Today is a rare, sunshiny day! Oh, it is so good to be alive.
I hung the baby's wash out this morning, there was such
a nice crisp breeze blowing. I wish I could describe
how delicate and peaceful the wispy clouds looked as if they
were being swept across the vast expanse of blue sky
with an imaginary broom.

There is a tall damask rosebush framing the front doorway of
this dear little house. Wherever I live, I always want to have a
damask rose planted even if they are hard to grow in our area.
I can hardly wait to see what this one will look like once it is in
bloom. Why would someone give up such a charming place, I asked
Yosef; he told me the elderly woman who owned it died without
having any children.

Imma says this kind of rose will have exceedingly
wonderful fragrance. She also discovered
that Roman government officials like
to make wreaths of them. Oh, did I forget to tell you?
I am sending my diary to her as regularly as
possible, by caravan, which isn't regular at all. Oh, I long to see her
face once again and have her say a *Banoah, (blessing,)* over . . . my
own dear baby. I hope by then Abba will, will…never mind.

Let's see, I was talking about the rosebush.
I am eagerly watching for the first green leaf bud to uncurl.
They are quite literally thorn bushes right now and are very
handy for drying baby's swaddling clothes, and dry they will.
The way the naughty wind is whipping and snapping at them, I think
she wants to carry them over to the Aleichem's (neighbor's) place.

But what would a couple of bachelor brothers want with swaddling
clothes? Everyone teases them so for not getting married. I think finding
baby things on their doorstep would be quite infuriating to them.

We young *aant'at* have so much fun filling our stone
amphorae (vessels), and hauling water from the well.
We have decided to meet at day-break on the first day of
each week to scrub our laundry together. Somehow, a big
job doesn't seem so wearisome if you have friends doing
it with you.

DEAR DIARY,

I am taking a housewifely pride in how sparkling white these
swaddling clothes look in the sunshine,
but I am also concerned that the wind might be tugging holes into
the soft new cloth. Maybe I'll need to find another way to dry them.
Seeing them ripple in the sunshine reminds me of something *Rebbe
Jehosophat* preached about last Shabbat. I remember it fully.

*'But who may abide the day of His coming? And who shall stand
when He appears? He is like refiner's fire and fuller's soap. He shall
sit as a refiner, a purifier of silver, he shall purify the sons of Levi.'*

Who is this referring to? Could it actually be
my Son, my pure, innocent little boy.

Yeshua seems so pure and good. I know all babies are innocent,
but there is something about Him, or maybe it is
just knowing who He is that makes me want to tremble.
How will He be a purifier of the son's of Levi?
Why of Levi? Are they not generally more upright than
the rest because the priests spring from that tribe?

Did I ever tell you that *Yehoshua* means *Jehovah saves*?
It seemed like the right name for Him, yet we
wonder who He will save or how.
I know so very little about *Yahweh*,
compared to what there is to know,
yet *Elohim*: the Creator of the tremendous thunder clouds and
yellow lightning as well as every trembling, newborn Coney,

with their velvety, brown eyes, has given me the keeping
of His helpless Babe babe. I know right from the bottom
of my heart that I . . . we . . . meaning Yosef and I,
will both need to rely heavily on the Heavenly Father to
guide and direct us in this high and holy calling.

Just now, our little one opened His eyes and seemed to be looking
at me. Those eyes that saw the vast star dotted sky the moment it
was spoken into existence are now focused on me alone. Oh what a
tender-sweet look! Such clear, trusting eyes are gazing at me. I bent
over to smile at Him, my heart warmed with joy.

Will this Child someday be compared to refiner's fire or a fuller's
soap? If the effect He has on me already is any indication,
He certainly
could be. Just being with Him gives me such a prayerful longing
to be more sure, more tender and loving, more sweet and good,
more of everything that would be pleasing in His *Shekinah*.
Oh to be more like *El Shaddai*, the One who carries us in His arms.

7th Tevet

December 20th

DEAR DIARY,

A knock sounded at the portal just now. Just a tiny knock that I may not have heard, if I had not been about to sweep my small pile of dust out the door. Lo, a young lad stood upon my threshold and handed me a bulky parcel, which was wrapped in a fluffy white fleece.

"Oh, what a lovely lamb skin. *Yeshua* will be so cozy when He is snuggled up in it! And what are these?" I took the topmost clay tablet and examined it with an interested, yet quizzical gaze.

"Do you not know who I am?" he questioned with a disappointed air. Feeling reproached, I realized he was more than just an errand boy, being unsure of his identity, I felt reluctant to venture a guess.

"I am the son of the head shepherd who visited you in the cave."

Recognition dawned. The lamp had been so dim and smoky in that cavern; he had hung shyly towards the back, but now I recognized his fair youthful features.

"Although we are poor in earthly goods", he explained in a quaintly grown-up manner, "we longed to present a gift to the Christ Child."

"What is this all about?" I asked, holding up the tablet.

"It is our memories of the night the angels came to proclaim the glad news. My Abba wrote it!"

"Why thank you, thank you—"

"Joel, the name is Joel bar Abia."

"Thank you, Joel. Would you care for something hot to eat
before you go?" I had seen him eying
the steaming barley loaves resting beside pottery dishes of
freshly churned butter and a delectable honeycomb.

He shrugged his shoulder, reluctantly, I suppose, not
wanting to admit how hungry he actually was.
I knew it was a long way back to the hills where the shepherds had been
keeping watch over their flocks for the last several weeks, so I thrust
two freshly buttered loaves into his hands just as baby started to cry.

Joel watched eagerly as I went to pick up *Yeshua*.
Then he followed me inside and pressed his forehead against
the Baby's, tickled Him under the chin and with a boyish
hop, scurried out the door, headed towards the hills.

It is time to lay my reed pen down. Yosef will wonder why
there are only two barley loaves to go with our soup today.
I would hasten to make more, but the coals have grown cold and there is
no time. We will just have to make do today by having extra vegetables.

Same day...

DEAR DIARY,

The shepherds' story was so incredible! I read it to Yosef this evening
while he was whittling away at a handle for some sort of tool,
a bow-drill, I think.

Yea, once again I am thankful that my dohd
taught me to read. I think Yosef enjoyed the story also
and I noticed that his eyes were soft when he rose to
tuck the blanket about the infant's tiny frame.

We have no room to store the clay tablets in our single-room dwelling,
so I will be busy in the next few days transcribing them onto
parchment before storing them in the chest with
my diary and other precious scrolls. This will be a
hard job for me because I have never copied
another's writings before.

Remind me to mix up a new batch of ink. I am soon going to
run out. I prefer to make my own, since every little thing I do
to save money makes it easier for my hard working husband.

I, I, Abia, bar Dothan will now apply myself to writing down the memoirs of the shepherds' visit to the newborn King. The night I will tell you about will always be fixed in my memory with the slightest detail as clear as if it had but recently happened.

It had begun as a typical night for us shepherds, although colder than some, and those who were not stretched out on the grass fast asleep were huddled close to the fire chatting. Some of us had our young sons with us. Zeke has a trusty old *kelev*, (dog,) that most of us appreciate very much as he can faithfully make the rounds by himself. To my right, *Aron* was carefully pruning away on a twig in order to make a sharp point. For what purpose I knew not.

"So what do you think about the coming of the *Mashiach*, Judah," he asked?

Judah sighed heavily. "I only wish He would come. When the *Yisraelites* were in bondage to the Egyptians, they were their slaves for four hundred years before deliverance came. How long is it now since the prophet Malachi plodded where we plod? Four hundred years? *HaShem*, hallowed be His Name, is silent! We need another deliverer!" He glanced around quickly, then added, "The Roman taxes are too much to handle as it is, but," his voice lowered, "But it is the tithes that our religious leaders place on everything—absolutely everything that really drains us! No wonder so many of our brethren give up and join the hordes of bandits!"
"But we want to serve His Name faithfully!" *Aron* protested. "Even if that means tithing."
Judah was about to put him in his place with a heated word or two, but I quickly tried to mollify him.
"There was Judah the Maccabee, your ancestor," I pointed out. "He strove to do his part."
"Yea, and would to *HaShem* that he was here, now!" Judah snapped the stick that he had been peeling in half, and hurled both ends into

the fire. "I would raise up an army myself, but it seems so futile. Many a revolt has flared up, but those dastardly Romans quench it in no time! Their horrible crosses line the hills and roadsides."

We all looked down. Most of us were probably thinking about the disaster in Sepphoris not many years thence, and we dreaded the thought of it being repeated. That was one uprising that resulted in far too many horrible crucifixions.

Judah's chin jutted out, causing his thin, pointed beard to quiver as he glared at each one of us in turn.

"Think not that I am a coward because I am skulking around in these hills pretending to be a shepherd. They are ferreting out every son of the Maccabees as you well know, so we have to be sly. The time is not right."

None of us cared to disagree with him, nay, not with those fiery eyes boring into us.

We all fell silent. Some of us were inclined to stretch out on our backs; arms folded behind our heads and study the stars, others gazed meditatively at the glowing embers.

I was watching the movement of the sheep. Gradually, it dawned upon me that they were becoming increasingly agitated for such a peaceful night.

My son, Joel, broke the stillness with a comment; "We have been learning about the lights in school," he ventured shyly.

"Lights? What lights?" Zeke prodded some sticks deeper into the coals then hunkered down beside Joel.

I spoke up; "He's referring to the lights in the temple in the time of Judah of Maccabee."

Zeke's face brightened, in the flickering fire light I thought I saw lingering smiles soften several countenances.

"That was a miracle," Joel said. As his father, I could tell that my son continued to feel ill at ease, surrounded as he was by all of us rough, brawny shepherds.

Several heads nodded.

There was a relaxing of the atmosphere as we sat back, reminiscing about Judah and his father Matthias.

I am sure 'our' Judah was proud to be the descendant of
such brave and fearless warrior—leaders who valiantly
rescued *Yerushalayim* from the wicked Syrian-Greeks."
"I can almost picture their dismay, however, when they finally
slashed their way through to the temple, only to find it in
shambles." *Aron* sighed and poked idly at the embers;
"What must have shocked those battle-hardened soldiers the most
after all that fighting was to find that Jehovah's lamp had gone out
and they were able to find only enough pure oil to last for one day!"
"Yet, it lasted for eight days!"
Joel's good friend, Micah, piped up. There was a huge grin on his face.
"Until they were able to make more oil," another
little fellow added. We all nodded jovially.
"Is there some sig—sig-nif-ee-glance in light? "Micah
asked. I hid my grin behind my quivering mustache.
Micah always did love to use such ridiculously long words.
"It represents *HaShem*," I explained.
I had been keeping an eye on the *kelev*, dog while we talked.
He seemed restless and uneasy. Now, he sat down on his
haunches, and half whined, half whimpered at the sky.
Zeke arched his hand over his eyes. "Can't see any
strange prowlers out there . . . can you?" He unfolded
his long frame and ambled over to the *kelev*.
"Look at that!"
Joel breathed, pointing with a shaking finger.
Far in the distance, one star seemed to be hurtling
towards us. As it increased mightily in size, as one
man, we were pulled to our feet to stare at it.
Then we saw that it was the radiant form of a shiny white
being, an Angel from far beyond the starry skies.
Terrified, we prostrated ourselves on the ground,
and buried our faces in our arms.
As quickly as the fear overcame us, it was quenched by the
most majestic, yet beautiful, voice any of us had ever heard.
"Fear not, for I bring you good tidings of great joy which shall be to
all people." Fear not? I looked up timidly, yet expectantly, and then
the rest of what he said sank in.

What does he mean? All people? Blacks? Scythians? Greeks? Romans?
Gaul's, bond, and free? Or did he just mean Jewish people
and their Yisraelites brethren across the Euphrates, and
elsewhere? What a marvelous message we were receiving!

But wait! He is not done! We gazed upon each other with looks of
incredible joy as the angel explained how we would know it was true.

"For unto you is born this day in the city of David, a Savior which is
Christ the Lord." A Savior? In the City of David? That's Beth Lechem!!
"Come with me! We must go find him!"
But in the space of a heartbeat, before I could even utter those words,
the sky seemed to explode with a thousand twinkling lights;
in the blink of an eye they were transformed into the most
magnificent gathering of Angels that this world has ever seen.
I will never be able to comprehend why we poor, lowly shepherds were
given the privilege of hearing that awe inspiring celebration, but I
am telling you, we were sure thrilled.
It's a good thing that ole Zeke's *kelev* is a dependable critter,
because wild hyenas could not have kept us woolly shepherds
from rushing pell-mell into the city, trouping down the streets to find
where baby *Yeshua* lay. You should have heard the shouting an'
singing, an' general carrying on while we scurried over those hills.

It didn't last, though. Such a deep hush came over us when we
stooped to enter the cave, and followed the smoky trail of the poor
pilgrim's oil lamp. He lead us, we were almost on tiptoe, to
where the newborn Baby lay nestled in his weary, but happy mother's
arms. We all dropped to our knees in worshipful adoration.

You should have seen Judah as he held that small infant. The tears
trickled down his weathered, craggy cheeks and he kept murmuring;

"He's come; the Deliver has come."
All glory, praise, and honor belong to our great *Yahweh*
for allowing us the honor of worshipping His Newborn
Son. The Light of the world arrived on *Chanukahs*.

December 29th

DEAR DIARY,

So much has happened to us in the last several weeks.
Yeshua is growing into such a sweet, healthy little babe.
He pumps His arms and legs in such a beautiful, rhythmic fashion;
it is so enjoyable to watch that I leave him unbound occasionally.
I wrap him up snugly for sleeping, of course, because He seems to feel
more secure that way.

I am sure He recognizes me! How my heart throbbed with joy the
first time He turned and looked at me, and then actually smiled.
Our little *Yeshua* has such beautiful, luminous eyes.
It looks like they will be a startling green which is very
unusual among our people. It may seem strange to say
it about my own dear son, but I just adore Him.
Just being with and caring for Him is influencing me to reach
out to others with deeper kindness and compassion.

Part of me
wants to cuddle our little baby in my arms forever,
but another part of me longs to do
everything else just a little better in order to
please him and my precious husband.
I have noticed that even Yosef seems a little awed in His presence; he
holds Him gingerly, as if he's afraid He is too fragile for a clumsy man to
handle. Sure, I know a lot of first time Abba's act like that, but it seems
like it's even more so with him, or different somehow. The first
time I saw the Babe grow angry because I didn't feed Him as
soon as He thought I ought to, I relaxed, knowing
there was a human streak in Him!

It's no wonder though, that Yosef is so nervous, with
all the miraculous things that have happened.

When people ask to hold Him, they have no inkling that
He is a heavenly treasure and we have made a pact not to
talk about it. That's our little secret now and Yeshua's later
on, although we know not how it will be revealed
to Him. He will announce it as He sees fit . . . in Yahweh's good time.

Folks say, "What a lovely *tinoki,* or such a good baby," and
go on their way never knowing how blessed a Child they
have gazed upon. It makes me shiver to think about it.

5th Shevat

January 16th

DEAR DIARY,

Tomorrow, at sunrise, we will be making the journey to *Yerushalayim*. According to the Sacred Scrolls, all baby boys must be dedicated when they are forty days old.

6th Shevat

January 27th

DEAR DIARY,

There was only a pale streak of gray border at the bottom of the plum-
colored horizon when Yosef helped me
sit upon dear, faithful Balaam's back. *Yosef* pressed his lips against
the baby's soft, velvety cheek before handing Him to me.
Our eyes met in the semidarkness and he whispered;

"Be careful."

"I will."

After I tucked the end of my shawl around the little bundled baby
boy sleeping in my arms, we shared a moment of almost inaudible
prayer. Yosef took the reins and lead the way. As we plodded along
the dusty country road, I wondered what he was thinking about.

Yosef is a quiet sort of fellow, full of deep feelings, but not given to
much talking. I am so thankful that he is convinced that *Yeshua*
is the Son of God. At times he treats me with a respect
that borders on reverence and I feel myself blush.
Then I must sweetly remind him that I am only the vessel.
It is the Son in my arms that is the priceless treasure.

While we were yet betrothed, he was very troubled and
shrank back from me in a way that cut to my soul.
Gossips insinuated that I had been overtaken by a Roman
soldier. Sometimes they rampage our towns and all the women
flee into hiding. I've heard other stories even nastier.

Yosef was deeply troubled that the rumors might be true. I
am afraid he also worried at times that I had been unfaithful.
It makes tears course down my cheeks to think about it, let
alone write it, but I'll try not to have hurt feelings.

Even after he had that dream that he was supposed
to take me as his wife, I sensed a hesitancy,
but I know he prayed much about it and even fasted.
By the time little *Yeshua* came into the world, and such marvelous things
happened, he seemed to have firmly put all his doubts behind him.

"Oh, Yosef," I called, as we rode along, "I am so very thankful!"
Yosef turned back and looked at me in surprise.

"Thankful for what, *Chavivi?*"

"That you believed that *Yeshua* is the Son of *HaShem*!" He
walked over to me with the reins still in his hands and tilted
my chin with one finger in order to gaze into my eyes

"Mary'am, it wasn't that I was *unwilling* to believe."

We walked a few paces, I thought that was all he
was going to say but then he continued,

"I wanted to believe after the initial shock wore off.
Common sense reminded me what a sweet, tender-hearted
pleasant *talitha* you were always known to be."

We stopped, he took my hands in his big, square carpenter hands.
"I was worried about how our neighbours would respond."

"That is still hard to cope with," I said in a low trembling voice.

He leaned forward to kiss me tenderly. "But we will go forward, trusting *El' Shaddai*, hallowed be His Name, yes?"

I nodded mutely and leaned my head against his shoulder for a moment.

As we continued on our journey, I smiled softly to myself while admiring his strong, broad shoulders, the relaxed easy way he strode down the road. His influence has a steadying effect on me when I am overwhelmed at the implications of what has happened.

We have decided to break our fast at a scenic spot overlooking the trail. I am glad for the rest. We have been going mostly uphill for many furlongs now, or so it seems. The donkey needs a rest, also.

What makes it so nice is that there is a tiny stream trickling from a cleft in the rocks nearby. Such cold, clear water is so refreshing!

The sky has brightened considerably since we departed. There is faint smudge of pink in the vast expanse of azure blue.

The roads are becoming more congested with people leaving their houses to travel hither and yon, on foot or with all sorts of conveyances. I wonder what kind of heartaches our fellowmen have hidden beneath their bluster or reserve.

6th Shevat

January 17th

DEAR DIARY,

The donkey had just picked his way around some wild
oleander bushes that were loaded with pink flowers
when a cluster of screaming lepers burst into sight. They were yelling,

"Unclean! Unclean!"

We all scattered. I have never been that close to such
deformed people before. It was a gruesome sight.
Many of them were missing body parts, including noses, with
mere stumps for hands. Their skin was a sickly, pasty white, the
unnaturally harsh screech of their voices still rings in my ears.
My heart squeezed with pity even as I fled with the rest.

Later, I kissed our precious Yeshua's soft cheek and wondered
what His response will be when He is all grown up,
when He sees such a pathetic sight. Why is there so much
suffering in the world? Can nothing be done to stop it?

7th Shevat

January 18th

DEAR DIARY,

Although we had acceptable accommodations with relatives, I kept
tossing and turning on my straw mat. I finally got up to write in my
diary by the light of early, early dawn.
Pictures of those disfigured lepers kept crowding my mind. Leprosy!
What an awful, awful disease. What causes it, I wonder?
Can it truly be the result of uncleanness like some insist?
Then why is it that some of the most immaculate,
most respectable people get it?

I caught sight of a mother carrying a baby and I could have
cried while fleeing. A baby! In such dire circumstances. *Oh
El Shaddai*: I wept, *no! Please no! Not an innocent baby!*

Yosef seemed surprised that I would be so broken up about
the state of the lepers. Some think they are worthy
to be despised and rejected of men. I can hardly bear
the thought of seeing them on the way back.
Nay, but on the other hand, I hope Yosef will allow me to purchase
some extra victuals in case we do see them. I want to give them
something nourishing to eat and maybe a wee garment for the baby.
It seems like such a little thing to do, but I
think *El' Shaddai* would be pleased.

We went to the temple sometime in the early afternoon,
Yosef purchased two turtledoves for the sacrifice.
They were such pretty little things, they cooed so sweetly. It made my
heart ache that they had to sacrifice their lives because of my sins.

After Yosef tethered the donkey, I clung to his arm. It is
frightening being jostled among the teeming multitudes
on the busy streets of *Yerushalayim*. What would I
do if I was to get separated from my *chavivi?*

Entering the temple was a new experience entirely.
I was somewhat prepared for the vastness of the building but its
glory was disgracefully marred by the animals in the temple. It
was appalling to see livestock milling around in *El Elohim*'s Holy
House, leaving you-know-what all over the place! It is supposed
to be a sacred place meant to magnify The Most Holy One.

I could hardly stand to see the Holy Temple desecrated so!
It's easy to imagine the appalled look on
King Solomon's face if he saw it. How does *Yahweh*
feel about such disgusting practices?
Why can't the money changers go elsewhere to do their
business? The Gentiles will never want to worship in the
outer court with this going on, and yet some of us are
willing for them to become proselytes if they so desire.
I know it may seem silly, but I hugged my dear, little boy
closer and covered His eyes because I was loath to let him
see what they had done to His Father's House.

Yosef was still edging his way through the congestion
so I could not stand and stare. I scurried after him
and hoped he knew where he was going.

Just as a Levite accepted our meager offering, I saw a darling lamb
which was about to have its throat slit by another Levite who
would drain its blood into a bowl. I turned to Yosef, feeling ill.

"Oh Yosef, must it be so?" I moaned, pressing my head for a brief instant against his sleeve. He gave my hand a sympathetic squeeze but continued talking with the priest.

My eyes seemed riveted to the tragic scene, and I bleakly realized that this sober deed is repeated more than a thousand times every Passover. The poor spotless lamb gave one low gurgling sound, then went limp.

I pressed my darling infant closer to my heart as my tears dampened his downy hair. I wiped them with His soft blanket and eventually gained control. It is so very painful to think of a lamb cutting short his wee perfect life for someone as sinful and undone as I.

8th Shevat

January 19th

DEAR DIARY,

I can't wait to tell you what else happened at the temple yesterday. It
was so strange and unexpected. Several young mothers were standing
around visiting while waiting to dedicate our babies to *El Shaddai*. I
kept a close eye on Yosef.
I cared not to get separated from him in that crowd.
He was standing by a pillar, engaged in conversation with
a scholarly-looking gentleman, who must have been
close to the age of my father.
It surprised me at first that he could get involved in such deep
discussions, but then I remembered how he loves to pour over the
Torah and various prophecies at the dawn of each new day.
I will have many questions of my own to
discuss with him in the coming days.

I enjoy listening to mothers swapping baby stories, today was
no exception. Having a baby really draws *aant'at* close!

Did you happen to notice that I said listening instead of
sharing? Well, it's because the events surrounding
Yeshua's birth are so wonderful; I am cautious about
sharing them lest people would think
I am bragging. Nay, that is not all of it.
These events seem so special, I feel almost a reverent awe when
I meditate on them, and I do not want to trot them out for
just anybody to casually analyze or worse yet, belittle.
While we were chatting, an elderly gentleman hobbled
over to us, leaning heavily on his walking stick.
His flowing white beard nearly touched the
knobby hand that clutched the cane.

I watched with concern lest some rowdy young boys that were racing past would send him sprawling, but they managed to deftly sidestep him, just in time.

This aged grandfather came over to us, gently cradled each of our tiny babies in his arms, and gazed lovingly into his or her innocent, young eyes. A temple assistant held his cane, supporting his arm, as if he was quite used to these occurrences.

It was whispered from ear to ear that this was Shimon. He came to all the dedications as if looking for someone. Of course the other sisters were mystified but I bit my lip.

Just then Shimon lifted baby *Yeshua* from my arms and uttered such a gasp that I worried that something had gone wrong with his heart. his next words dispelled my concern.

"Oh Lord, blessed be your name!" he cried, touching *Yeshua* on his soft cheek."Lord, now let your servant depart in peace according to your word."

"Why does he say that?" The young mother next to me whispered. "He didn't say that when I had my first *riba.*"

I shrugged my shoulders but a strange feeling gripped my heart as hungrily I drank in every word he was saying.

"I have seen with my own eyes the salvation which you have prepared before the face of all people. He is a light to lighten the Gentiles and the Glory of Your people Yisrael."

My lips parted in amazement as I stared along with everyone else at that peacefully sleeping bundle in his arms.

Then Shimon turned to Yosef,
who had stepped to my side, and gazed solemnly at
us through his wise, kindly yet aging eyes.
After he placed the baby back in my arms, Shimon rested one frail hand
on my shoulder and one on Yosef's, while everyone watched intently.

"Behold," he intoned in a clear voice, "This *riba* is set for the fall, and
rising again of many in Yisrael, for a sign which shall be spoken against."

I vaguely sensed that the crowd was shrinking
back as different voices started muttering.
"Why is he speaking so strangely?"
"Is it a prophecy?"
"Is the old man touched in the head?"
Shimon continued regardless of the comments of those
around him. He looked me squarely in the eyes.
"Yea, and a sword shall pierce through your own soul also."

Out of the corner of my eye, I happened to see the priest lift
his knife to slay another lamb just then, the combination
of Shimon's words, with the death of the Lamb,
caused my heart to constrict. I tried to swallow a dry lump
of fear in my throat but it would not go down.

.

Even now, as I record these happenings of the day, my heart wants to
pound erratically.. *A sword shall pierce through your own soul also.* Why
did such an awful feeling, almost like a premonition, come over me
when he said that while I was watching the lamb being slain? Does
it relate to *Yeshua?* Nay, I will not go there. I cannot, I will not!

I just remembered the tail end of his thought; "that the thoughts
of many hearts may be revealed." What does that ever have to
do with me? I do not have an inkling! But oh I am so afraid!
Oh Yosef, *I need you to hold me close! I need you to hold
US close. Oh Yahweh, put your protective arms around
this little family! The future looks so dark.*

DEAR DIARY,

I was so shook up last night by what Shimon had declared that I forgot
all about the other thrilling thing that happened.

Scarcely had Shimon shuffled away when a very
old lady came scurrying over to us.
Her dark eyes were bright with laughter, she fairly snatched
the baby out of my arms, raising him high in the air.
She was delighted to see the infant and told everyone who
would listen about him. I do not recall what she had to say
but Yosef and I gave each other long, thoughtful looks.
Somehow, we just knew our future, and especially the baby's,
was going to be very eventful.

I clung to Yosef's elbow as we found our way out of the temple.
He had the baby positioned over his shoulder
and I leaned slightly against his arm, even though
couples are not supposed to show affection in public: the
rules are much stricter in Judea than in Galilee.
I am almost ashamed how much confidence I
put in Yosef as my leader and guide.
Should I not trust in *Yahweh* more?
Maybe someday when I am older and wiser I will understand
Adonai better, and it will be easier to put my trust in Him,
but for now I am so glad I have Yosef to lean on.
After all, I am so young, yet, I still have very much to learn.

9th Shevat

January 20th

DEAR DIARY,

It is late at night, the stars are brilliant against a dark sky. I was awakened by the sweet calling of my little 'lamb' who was feeling hungry. We cuddled for a while as he nursed himself back to sleep. It is so comforting to hold him in the crook of my arm.

Yosef rarely notices when I get up to tend to *Yeshua's* needs,
I try not to let it bother me but sometime it does.
He is such a hardworking carpenter, sometimes
having to lift heavy beams of wood and such;
I'm thankful when he can get good night's sleep.
Sometimes he is restless at night because of some sort of
pain in his chest. Hopefully, it's nothing serious.

I lay there thinking about when my small son is all grown up.
Will He be a famous king and sit on an golden throne
while ruling the nations of the earth? Will people from
all around the world heap honors upon Him?

If so, how am I, an unlearned young *aant'at*, supposed to prepare
Him, the son of the Almighty *HaShem*, hallowed be His name,
for such a tremendous task? It puzzles me,
why did *Yahweh* choose a simple country maid for such outstanding
responsibility? Of course He knew what He was doing,
but I am not sure if I do. Will He be an Earthly King? Or is there
something else in His future that we can't quite understand?

I suppose, since I am His mother,
I will also be honored.
At least that is what cousin Elisheva claims.
But what about poor Yosef?
Perhaps he will remain in the shadows all his life, but that isn't fair.
How could I ever manage so much responsibility if he doesn't continue
to support and believe in me . . . in us, down through the years?

Picturing *Yeshua* being crowned king nearly takes my breath away
but what about those prophetic words of old Shimon,
yea, a sword shall pierce through your own heart also.
Will He be killed in war?
I see that I have been clenching and unclenching
my fists until the knuckles gleam white,
but I have one more question.
Will I ever be welcomed into my Abba's home again?

Ah my, so many questions, so few answers.

23rd Shevat

February 3rd

DEAR DIARY,

Life has settled into a quiet but happy routine now that we are
home from our eventful trip to *Yerushalayim*. I really enjoy simple
homemaking and the privilege of being a mother to our precious baby.
He is such a pleasure to care for.

Akeret Ha-Bayet. Akeret Ha-Bayet
is what my *Mimi* used to always say. Aye, it is true
that women are the foundation of the home,
but oh, what a responsibility.
We surely need to lean on *Adonai*, hallowed be His
Name, and our husbands for guidance.

Now on to a different topic: the young *aant'at*, who are my age
here in Beth Lechem, are less haughty than the ones in Navara.
Maybe it is because they have not heard any suspicious
rumours regarding how *Yeshua* came into this world. I long
to believe they would be kind to me even if they had.
I think most of us look forward to meeting at sunrise at the village
well when we go to fetch water for our daily needs. It is a chance to
socialize.
Ruth, especially, has become a dear friend.
Remember when I said I wished that Ruth from
olden times could have been my friend?
Well, I think *this* Ruth must have very much the same
character that I imagined that Ruth would have had.
Later on in the day, we often meet at the old sycamore tree
nearby and go to the market. Sometimes Lydia or one of the
other young *aant'at* coincides her shopping with ours,
we have such an agreeable time together. It is so amusing watching
Ruthalei's little boy, Benoni, caper along ahead of us.

He is such a cunning little fellow. We often try to hide
our smirks behind our hands lest he realize how amused
we are at his antics, lest he begin to show off.
Lydia is another special friend. Her daughter, Mariamme,
is as sweet as an angel. She is about one year old, she has
delightful dimples and winsome big brown eyes.
Some day we expect to go back to Navara again, I will
miss these friends. But we will wait until *Yeshua* is sturdy
enough to handle the travelling reasonably well.
It's not that I do not look forward to seeing my
family once more, because I do, but those last several
months were clouded with difficult memories.

Yet I do understand why they treated me so coldly.

1st Adar

February 11th

DEAR DIARY,

Today was such an ordinary day, but it is the very ordinariness of it that I love so much. The simple routine of cooking, cleaning and caring for my family is so rewarding. I'm so thankful that I can be a wife and a mother.

2nd Nisan

March 13th

DEAR DIARY,

It is a whole year since I felt *Adonai's Shekinah*
surrounding me in such a hallowed way.

A whole year, and how my life has changed! I feel like I have
grown so, being the mother of *Yeshua* has done much for me.
It has definitely deepened my love
and respect for *Adonai*, and makes me want to be more caring.

Even though my life is quiet and peaceful, I want
to include here a little word picture of my days. Having a baby is helping
me to see my daily routine with new eyes, much like He may see it.
Yeshua gazes all around wonderingly and I like to
try to guess what He might be thinking.

Just as the dawning sun casts a glow over the distant hills,
Yosef chooses a scroll from the chest in the corner. This
is generally the most serene, blessed part of the day.

He reads something from one of the prophets,
the books ascribed to *Moshe* or perhaps a proverb or two.
We often sing one of the
Psalms of our father, David, and share what's on
our hearts before kneeling in prayer.

While he gets started in the attached carpenter shop,
I build a small fire in our round clay oven, then
mix and knead the daily batch of bread.
There is something so pleasant about kneading and turning
the dough each morning. Later, I will use the wide, smooth paddle
that my husband carved for me to place the loaves near the coals.

Later still, as we *aant'at* stroll outside the gate
to get our daily supply of water,
neighbours from nearly every house on various streets join us.

We worry because Aisha is not coming out.
She has been sick for so long.
When will her married daughter arrive from
Khirbet Qana (Cana) to help her
and how will the daughter manage to care for her
Imma with those twin toddlers underfoot,
and another one coming soon?

It is unspoken knowledge that Lydia will be carrying
extra water today as usual so that Aisha, her nearest
neighbour, will have some for her own needs.

We are such a variety of Galilean sisters. Some are stooped
and graying, always swathing themselves in severe, usually
faded black, attire. Others are as young, lively as we.

Sometimes, there are *zonahs* in their gaudy
apparel traipsing down the street,
but we rarely if ever meet them at the well.
They make us feel uncomfortable, maybe it works the other way also.

Leah has more than the average rolls of fat on her chin and
elsewhere, but her best friend Kutura is ever so tall and bony.
They are both jolly and friendly;
they and the five children between them keep things lively and amusing.

I had not realized until I decided to write this memoir
how much we three young married ones
tend to draw closer to each other and shrink away from
Haghaar when she strides over to the well.

She speaks sharply against the frivolousness of
young mothers of this day and age
and has brought poor Lydia to tears more than once,
with her stern criticism.
I don't know if we can do anything that would win her approval.

Lydia is by nature a giggly young Imma and can get
carried away sometimes with her exuberant ways,
but she's just so much fun to be with.
I hope *Haghaar* will not be too sharp with her today.

We ended up lingering a little too long outside the
gates by the well, so we had to hurry back.
My dough had risen nicely by then, I deftly formed it into
buns before using my paddle to place them into the oven.

The embers were just right, so I removed the ashes
and placed the loaves on the bricks inside our large clay oven,
which will remain hot enough until they are nicely done. Now
the bread will slowly bake and I will enjoy the homey aroma
while going about my other duties.
Fragrant, crusty bread hot from the oven is a taste I will never
grow weary of, especially if it is wheat instead of barley,
which we buy only for special occasions.

After replacing the dome-shaped cover,
I scurried about doing other things, stacking the pallets neatly
in the corner and sweeping carefully into all the corners
with my fine new broom.
After swishing the dust out the backdoor, I
hurried down the street to meet Lydia.

Since tomorrow is our day of rest, we needed to get all our shopping
and other work done quickly, before the first stars appear.
I met Ruth and Lydia, we wandered down the narrow,
dusty streets chatting companionably.

Old *Ozias* loves to haggle over the price of fish, he would be quite
disappointed if we did not passionately dispute with him.
Today, after lively debate,
I was able to get some fine dried *mousht,* a type of fish for our
Shabbat eve supper, at a price that I am sure will make Yosef happy.
As I turned into our yard,
my five colorful chickens rushed out to greet me, cackling loudly.
I exclaimed in dismay over forgetting to feed them,
just then baby *Yeshua* added to the general
racket with His 'hungry' cries.

Lydia giggled without mercy and retraced her footsteps, back to
her own door, while Mariamme snoozed contently on her back,
her thumb sweetly nestled in her mouth.

The day, which had begun so clear and cool waxed hot,
so I was glad for a chance to sit in our cool house a
few minutes later while feeding the baby.

He snuggled in my arms as songs of joy bubbled from my lips, snatches
of the prophecy that came to me while visiting Aunt Elisheva.

> **The Mighty One has done**
> **marvelous things to me; holy is His name . . .**
> **For He that is mighty**
> **hath done to me great things:**
> **and Holy is His name.**

I am so blessed. I must be the happiest woman alive. My little one
was as contented as a lamb, peacefully sleeping. I knew I would
soon have to put Him down but oh, I love holding Him!

While nursing the baby, I nearly dozed off to the peaceful sound of grinding. The women in the doorways of nearly every house in sight were busy grinding grain for their bread. There is companionship in having friends and neighbours all around.

After resisting the urge to sleep for a bit, I was soon kneeling beside my own millstones. While I poured grain into the hole in the centre and pushed the handle back and forth, my thoughts drifted. My sister, Hanalei, and I used to do this job regularly together. Our movements became so rhythmic that we could continue chatting amiably and scarcely notice what we were doing. I do not know how many times one or the other of us would reach for one more handful of grain only to find out it was empty. We would be still smiling while one of us held and jiggled our copper sifter, while the other poured the grain into it. How I miss those pleasant sisterly moments. Perhaps someday I will invite one of my friends to come over and we can share in this daily task.

Bear with me, my dear diary, if I skip lightly over the rest of the day. I will bore my dear Imma to tears if I dwell on all the mundane details. I will dance right into the evening because this one was special!

"Mary'am!" Yosef called, peering around the corner of the door. "Do you have a free moment? It is such a lovely evening. I was wondering if you could step outside to enjoy it with me." "Yes, my lord. After I finish drying the dishes and put them back on the shelf, I will be at your side."

Soon, we were standing on the doorstep, with Yosef's arm
was around my waist, my head resting on his shoulder.
It gives me such a secure feeling to be in his arms.
We listened to the lively sounds of a village finishing off its
day as we gazed at one especially bright star in the sky.

****

"Anna, there is one last hen crouched under that bush over there.
Fetch her in for the night, will you? David, please help her."

"Rebecca, this milk has a fly in it. You've got to be
more careful!" Rebecca's mother scolded.
"Tobias, stop pulling that dog's ears. He might bite you!
"Don't come crying to me. I warned you!"
"Get that scamp out of the house! You know that I don't allow
goats in here in warm weather. They are too rambunctious. Look,
she has knocked over a jug and the water has spilled. What a mess.
What were you thinking to let her in here without tying her?"
"But she's my pet. I like her!" someone whined in a shrill, child's voice.
"Nonsense! Out, Hexie, out! Now we will need
to go to the pottery shop for another—"
We heard a door slam shut, Yosef and I shared a small grin.

After Rebecca, her mother, Tobias, and a few others trouped
into their respective shelters, the evening seemed even
lovelier. Quieter for sure, so sweet, and fresh smelling.
We had received a shower earlier in the evening.

I glanced idly at the chicken tracks patterning
our path with their unique designs.

The rainy season is almost over, the hills, bathed now with
the golden glow of evening, look so luxuriant and gorgeous.
Poppies and many nameless varieties of flowers blossom by
the millions, their fragrance lingers along the streets.

We listened to one last mother call her son in for the
night and we watched as his shadowy form scampered
homeward with a small, *kelev* barking at his heels.

Then all was still.

After a while, Yosef pointed out an unusually bright
star in the heavens, we gazed at it together.

"Doesn't it remind you of *the* 'star' the shepherds saw which
turned out . . . not to be a star at all . . . but angels?"

I nodded silently. *Will this star mean anything special?*
A nippy little breeze came up which started me to
shivering so I snuggled a little closer to my man.

"I wonder how those shepherds are doing?" I mused. "It seems
like they could never be the same after such an exciting night."
"Seems like I will never be the same, either," Yosef mused.
I nodded soberly, then stiffened at the sound of a from within the house.
It did not come again so I continued to watch the brilliantly studded sky.

I noticed that Yosef's face was drawn, so I looked at him, hoping
he would share whatever was bothering him. At length he did.
"I feel so inadequate," he confided.

"Why so, *Chavivi?*" I asked, gently stroking his soft beard. I
saw emotion working on his face before he responded.

"What is my responsibility? How am I to raise
Him? He is *El' Shaddai's* Son! Not mine."
He groaned, then added, "I feel so useless!"
"Oh, but Yosef you are His Abba; his earthly father.
He will need you just as much as He needs me."
Yosef's strong broad shoulders sagged. "But how shall I teach—
instruct—the Son of *Hashem*?" His voice dropped to a whisper;
'Hallowed be His Name. *Elohim* has so much power. He created
the stars—the moon-—and the ground we walk on!'`

Yosef shook his head worriedly, my heart reached out to him.
"Yosef, just love, us . . . care for us, and with *Adonai's*
help the rest will somehow fall into place.'`

Yosef showed a glimmer of a smile,
I think, or at least hope, his mood lightened. The star
continued blazing brightly in the darkened sky, but we were
weary from a long day of work so we retired for the night.

Marilyn Friesen

2nd Iyyar

April 12th

DEAR DIARY,

Oh, my, oh my, what a commotion. What a surprise. What an incredibly different day! I woke up from all the noise, instantly wondering what had happened. There seemed to be a tremendous uproar going on.

My first (irrational) thought was that every mule in the village had gathered just outside our door to bray us a raucous good morning.

But it wasn't only mules. There was the sound of an unusual number of men shouting commands and what not to each other . . . in a foreign tongue, yet!

That caused me to rush out of bed in my slip of a night garment and fly to the window. What I saw caused me to fumble frantically into my newest Shabbat robe, to try to hastily restore a semblance of order to my unruly tresses. While I was thus occupied, Yosef, already dressed, was striding to the door with an almost stern expression on his chiseled good-looking features.

As my heart pounded into my throat, or so it seemed, I peered on tiptoe through our high window, as Yosef greeted some foreign strangers who were mounted on the most magnificently bedecked camels I've ever seen. The whole street and the one beyond was overflowing with their personal entourage. I shrank back in trembling amazement, wondering, *What could this mean?*

Without a doubt, this royal party had come from a great distance, but why were they coming to our humble door?

Yosef most courteously beckoned them to come in. I am certain
he must have felt like bowing to them, decked as they were in such
royal apparel, but it is our custom to bow to no man, only *Yahweh*.

I scurried back to our room and quickly combed out my
tangles; then I[D1] slipped out of our curtained-off sleeping
chamber. I was too nervous to don a robe of gracious dignity,
but hopefully those powerful magi didn't notice.
Immediately, the leader stepped up to me and clasped my hands in his.
"We have come to worship the newborn King,"
he said simply, "for we have seen His star in the east."
I felt the color wax and wane in my cheeks, yet my heart
thudded with joy. *Yea, verily, that is why they came. It
is not about us. It is about Him. It I about Jesus.*

After courteously excusing myself,
I went to get the baby. He looked so sweet with
His sleepy eyes and rosy cheeks.

All three of the men reached out to Him,
although I doubt if any of them had held babies much before.
They changed their minds and in humble adoration, dropped
to their knees instead. It brought tears to my eyes
to see these men of power and wealth bowing
low before the *tinoki* in my arms.

Yosef brought me a wooden stool,
I sat down with the baby on my lap and the Babe reached
out and stroked the head of one of the men.
He may have just been entranced by the glittering jewels on
his crown, but it seemed almost like a touch of blessing.
I felt a lump in my throat.
My own eyes were moist when I saw the tears streaming down the
tanned weathered cheeks of those exceedingly influential men.

They reverently took the Babe in their arms, He,
in turn would pat their cheeks or tug a little at the front of
their vestures. Yeshua has never felt a fear of strangers,
this time was no exception.
He was quiet in their arms, yet cheerful. I could tell they
could not get enough of Him. It reminded me anew what a
priceless treasure and responsibility was in our keeping.

They stayed around for a while, quietly talking of their journey,
although I could tell their eyes rarely roved from the face of Yeshua.

It was my impression, although they never said so in
so many words, that one was from Ethiopia, probably
a descendant of Queen Magda of Sheba;
another was almost certainly from Parthia, one of the royalties
from among our Yisraelites brethren who reside there; and the
other an Arabian, whose ancestor was Avraham's son, Ishmael.

It awes me to think that a star brought them all together,
leading them directly to our humble abode,
here in Galilee.
I did not glean many details
of whom they were because they were not inclined
to boast of their own credentials while basking in the *Shekinah*
of the Holy Son of *HaShem!*

I leaned forward, enthralled,
as they discussed many different prophecies that related to the
Mashiach, speculating how His life might proceed from here. Sitting
in the synagogue, hearing the most revered *rabbi* speak, could not
have made a deeper impression on me than that early morning visit.
Yosef was able to ask thoughtful questions,
which was a comfort to me because it is not becoming for a
woman to be inquisitive in the presence of a man other than her
husband. I am eager to learn more about Yeshua's future role.

As they lingered, I drew my veil around me as a sign of
womanly submission to their authority, yet began to worry
about the servants who were waiting outside.
I knew they must be weary and worn.
Those tending the animals and personal effects would
surely be feeling the rising heat of the day.
Should I slip out and offer them cups of cold water?

But then I recalled, I had not even fetched any for our own
use today, even if I had both our jugs filled to the brim,
it would not suffice for all the men to get more than a swallow
each. *And what about the poor, dumb creatures?* Ah, such a crowd
must have their own water supply, hopefully freshly refilled.

While my mind was thus wandering, the conversation
turned to other things.
During a lull, the tallest of the three noble gentlemen
rose and went to the door.
He beckoned to some of the servants who bowed low
several times while carrying some magnificent gifts.
A look of humility enhanced Yosef's features as they unwrapped
the gifts before *Yehoshua,* the new-born King. What
priceless treasures they were, symbolic also.

Did the gold represent kingliness? The frankincense,
which I believe comes from a tree in Africa, is probably a
reminder of His future religious authority and the beautiful
fragrance of His holy nature, but the myrrh, the myrrh,
I did not even want to look at it. It is used in the embalming of
dead bodies! Surely, it has other uses, unknown to me. Is He going
to be cut off in the prime of life? I pray not! But why, why did
Shimon tell me a sword would pierce through my own soul also?

I subconsciously linked fingers with Yosef's while the gifts were being
presented, then quietly waited as the wise men backed away, while
bowing low, towards the entrance.

It was high noon by the time the last donkey boy
trotted away behind the last pack animal.
We stood in the doorway and watched in silence.
Hardly had those at the head of the train entered the next
street when all of our neighbours poured out of their houses and
gawked after them. Before they had a chance to rush over,
and ask us a dozen questions, Yosef firmly shut the door
and put the bolt in place to give us some privacy.

We were not very hungry so I laid out only
a simple snack of goat cheese and leftover fava beans for our lunch
before settling down for a nap with Yeshua cradled in my arms.
I was dreaming that those men in their bright, silken garments
were running around the house looking for appropriate
hiding places for those expensive gifts,
but was startled to wakefulness by a knock at the door.

It was Lydia and Ruth. I had never seen them so excited,
so agitated before! Lydia, typically is more excitable, but it
was Ruth's anxiety that really caught my attention.
"What did those wealthy men want?"
Ruth demanded, even as I was opening the door.
Everyone is talking about it!" Lydia interrupted.
"Auntie Eunice said she counted at least twenty-five assistants
before she lost track because of the jostling of the animals!"`
"Why did they come to your door?" Ruth demanded.
"Were they spies or something? I thought Parthia was at peace
with Rome. But what would they want with you? …You!"
I tried to explain why they came and Lydia's eyes grew wider
and wider, but Ruth clenched her fists against her mouth.
I could see that Lydia was ready to bolt
out the door and spread the fabulous story to anyone and
everyone who would listen. I grabbed her sleeve.

"Don't go, Lydia. Don't!"
She whirled back, "Why not?"

"Don't spread the news about what happened not yet.
It's too special… too sacred."
She looked disappointed, but reluctantly nodded.
Then I turned to Ruth.
"Why are you so upset?" I asked softly.
She was staring fixedly at her little boy.
Benoni was crouching beside baby Yeshua, patting His hand.
My *chavivi* was lying on a rush mat, kicking His feet,
happy to have someone to play with.

Ruth turned abruptly to me, her voice was most
intense, "Oh Mary'am, I am so afraid!
Those rich famous men coming to our little town can only mean
trouble. I feel it in here," she pressed her hand against her bosom.

I wanted to talk her out of the notion but refrained because
of her ghastly complexion and her convincing manner
. I tried to comfort her with a hug but she was
too apprehensive to respond.
Without meaning to be naughty,
Benoni, out of curiosity, poked Yeshua's eye..
Yeshua briefly cried. I scooped Benoni into my arms.
Almost hungrily, Ruth reached for her little fellow.
"He did not mean to hurt the baby," I said, stroking His
fine light hair. "See, Yeshie has forgotten already,
He is trying to fit His foot into His mouth."
Ruth smiled, but barely. "Well, I guess I should go now,"
she sighed.
"Say bye-bye to Auntie," I said, planting a kiss
on Benoni's round smooth cheek.

He waved exuberantly and smiled, showing all three
of his tiny white teeth. I walked over to Lydia,
who was waiting impatiently at the door, and clasped Mariamme
in my arms for a moment before giving her back. She dimpled up
at me, then snuggled her head against her mother's shoulder.

Ruth's fear seemed to be catching, the glory of the day dimmed somewhat as I thought of all that she had said. *Could they be spies? What a ridiculous thought! Why would spies come to our house?* I glanced over at Yeshua, He had managed to flip over unto His tummy. *But He is a king . . . Who would not want another king to be born? Caesar Augustus? King Herod? Who? Who? The Parthian ruler?*

Nay, it cannot be! Now it was I who was feeling agitated. With swift practiced movements, I scooped up the happy little infant and put Him in a sling on my back.

It was high time the goats got milked, and the eggs collected. As I crossed the yard, I could see my friends trudging past the neighbours' houses. Benoni was scampering ahead, pausing every moment or two to sniff at a flower or pick up a stone, and in his funny little way, throw it.

Oh Yahweh," I whispered. There was a catch in my throat and I couldn't seem to go on. *What means this nameless dread that has suddenly darkened the day?* The chores got done, although I seemed to be functioning woodenly. After that, I stood and stared at the gifts displayed on the low table for a long time, deep in thought. Without really knowing why, I rewrapped them in their fine satiny coverings, then sewed them tightly into rough but sturdy burlap. Tonight, after Yosef has his supper, I will ask him to bury them deep under the house, to conceal the spot by putting our vessels of stored food and oil on top. Hopefully, they will be safe until such a time as Yeshua would need them.

At suppertime, Yosef was still animated about the morning's visit, he spoke about it between mouthfuls of his favorite lentil stew. At length, he took note of my solemn expression

and asked about it. When I told him about the
aant'at's visit, and how worried Ruth was,
his brows knit together.
He finished eating in silence. I longed to know what he was
thinking but refrained from asking. He would tell me
if he felt I needed to know.

DEAR DIARY,

I have not been sleeping soundly of late,
and it is not because Yeshua is teething.
For a young *aant'at,* one who has always been a sound
sleeper, this is highly unusual. I know that if Imma knew, she
would concoct some sort of herbal drink for me to sip before
going to bed, but she is too far away. (*Right,* Imma*?)*

Oh, dear, even just mentioning Imma
makes me teary-eyed.
It is so long since I have worked alongside her,
seen her sweet look of affectionate approval.

But that is also not what has been keeping me awake nights. Not
recently, at least. Ruth has been so nervous, fidgety for the last
two weeks, so much so that I have become troubled as well.

Benoni has a slight cold and she will not take him anywhere because
of it, not even to the community well! When she must go on an
errand, she begs her younger sister to watch over him, then
scurries back as quickly as possible.
Some of the others poke fun at her.
I do want to be sympathetic,
but when the sky is so bright, the babies adorable,
and our gardens are springing up in such wee tiny
rows, it's hard not to be enthused about life.

Lydia, poor wench, is usually such a happy person,
but I can tell she is being affected by Ruth's moodiness also.
Usually, she lets Mariamme toddle all over by herself, within
seeing distance of course. She used to allow her to pat any
strange *kelev*s, (dogs) she came across because they were
so gentle with the tot, but she doesn't any more. I hope Ruthalei''s
blue mood will soon lift so we can get on with the enjoyment of life.

Benoni is prattling so much now. He must have learned ten new
words in the last week or two! I told Ruth just this morning,

"Ruthalei, just relax, enjoy your son."
She looked down, but didn't answer.

My radishes are up, every one of them, so are the leeks. It is so
exciting. This is the first time I am having my very own garden. It is
so much more fun having *my own* than doing it for someone else.

Baby Yeshua is able to sit up very nicely. All too soon, He will be
scooting all over the place, then look out! I want to enjoy every
single moment of His infancy and His childhood because they
are so fleeting, and He is such a sweet, precious little *tinoki*.

15th Tishri

October 1st

DEAR DIARY,

It has been several months since the rich, powerful Magi
came to worship Yeshua.
Ruth is more herself again.
I am so relieved! I still think about the Magi's visit a lot, and I pray
every single day that I can be the kind of mother that *Adonai* wants me
to be for His own tiny *tinoki* who can crawl around so quickly now.
It seems like such a considerable responsibility to both
of us as His parents, but Yeshua is such a sweet *tinoki*,
it is impossible to get too burdened down.

Lydia shared a new idea for preparing chicken with me this morning. It
sounds so delicious. She mixes honey and mustard together. Then she
rubs it on the cut-up pieces just after they are cooked, then places
them on the bricks inside the oven until they are browned.

We only butcher a hen when guests are expected (we have
only one rooster left, he's not going anywhere!).

I will try this recipe on *Chanukah* because Abba and
Imma hope to come visit us. I can hardly wait!

Hopefully, our brooding hen will soon have a
fine batch of chicks for us to raise.

I have been getting enough eggs to even sell some, so I have been
working on a lovely new frock for *Chanukah*. It's times like this
that I miss Imma and Hana the most because it brings back
memories, oh, how we would stand and weave together.

It is a special thing to get new clothes, though, and Yosef likes the colors I have invented in the past. I am trying to come up with two complementary shades of blue for this garment and may have to ask one of the cloth sellers in Sepphoris for advice, since the one in Navara doesn't make as good a quality of dye.

One chicken has been brooding on a nest of eggs
for over two weeks. I am very excited.
Soon, soon we should have a batch of fluffy new chicks. I can hardly wait to show them to Yeshua, to see how He will react. I know He is too young to understand, but I will tell Him anyway that His Heavenly Father created them to be so soft and cuddly because He knew we would love them that way.

DEAR DIARY,

My hands are shaking so badly, I can scarcely hold my pen.
I hope this will be legible. The most appalling, the very, very most
terrible thing has happened. It is very dark out, Yosef shook me awake
with an urgency that I have never seen in him before.

While I scribble, he is rapidly stuffing clothing and other
belongings into a saddlebag. Now he is hurling it out the door,
shoving our huge lentil pot out of the way in order to scrabble in
the dirt until he can retrieve the hidden treasures. He muttered
something about a dream. What am I doing, wasting time writing?
I must sign off now and prepare the baby for a midnight escape,
although I tremble to think where we are going and why.

17th Tishri

October 3rd

DEAR DIARY,

"Get up! Get up!" Yosef cried in a hoarse whisper, and practically dragged a frock over my head. I sleepily donned it as well as an outer garment, then out of habit reached for my writing supplies.

Yosef led, nay, nearly dragged me over to the donkey.
I managed to climb up by myself, he wrapped Yeshua
onto my back and quickly fastened two saddle bags.
He tied a blanket roll behind me, threw another blanket
over my shoulders and tucked one edge around
the baby.

He hurried off to fill a goat bag with water. After
tossing it to me, he nearly dragged the donkey through
some crooked back streets and out of the town.
By this time, I was thoroughly awake and frightened.
"Yosef" I called, "where are we going?"
"Shh!"
Now that hurt, but it bewildered me also.
Yosef has always been so kind to me, I could not understand
why he would retort so hastily to a simple question.

I wished I could fasten the water bottle somewhere
instead of carrying it, but we were going fast
and I was being jostled so miserably that it seemed impossible.
Just as I managed to get it hooked around a saddle horn, a
scream so chilling and blood-curdling pierced the air.
I nearly fell off the donkey.
Fortunately, Yosef, who had been looking back at that moment,
reached my side just in time to keep me from having a bad tumble.

He cradled me in his arms whispering,
"Are you alright?" I nodded weakly, he mumbled something
about, "We got to get out of here and fast," and rushed
ahead once again, with the reins in his hands.
I kept looking back, terrified. *Is there some kind of wild feline pacing us?*

Far in the distance, on the main cobblestone road
entering Beth Lechem, I saw the flashing gleam of metal. Not
just one flash either, nay, but a wavering stream of flashes.
It was so eerie, I was puzzled by what it could be. Then it hit me
like a rock. *Beth Lechem, dear, sweet Beth Lechem is under siege!*

Why would such a little town be under attack during these peaceful times?
I heard another scream, the sound seemed to ricochet all
around! Then I thought I heard—no, I did hear the cry—
the terrified wail of a baby, then of many little children.

Yosef was behind us now, franticly whipping
the donkey to get him running. The poor creature has never been treated
so brutally before. I leaned hard against Balaam's neck as he galloped,
I clung to him as if my life depended on it, which it most surely did.

What terrifying thing was happening behind us, how
did Yosef know enough to flee when he did?
He had said something about a dream but I could not think about it
now. It took all my concentration just to stay on the donkey's back,
and not focus on the pain of a little hand tangled in my hair.

Yosef do you know where we are going? It is a moonless night, I
couldn't see a path from up there ! We seemed to be heading into
trackless desert, my mouth was dry with thirst. Or was it fear?
Yeshua started to fret. My heart went out to him.
He must be miserable bouncing around so. I know I
was. The whimpers turned into lusty wails.

"Hush the baby!" Yosef gasped.

How could I? He was on my back. I tried singing a lullaby but it made
it even worse. Yosef kept looking back, I suspected his face was white
with anxiety, although it was too dark to tell. *What could I do?*
I simply had no idea how to comfort my *tinoki* and Yosef
was terrified that something might happen to the Son
of the Holy One and he would be responsible!

"Yosef can't we stop for but a moment?" I pleaded,
"Beth Lechem is far in the distance."

He kept on and Yeshua's wailing increased in crescendo.

Finally, he halted, looked at me and pulled at his hair.

"Please, my lord, if I nurse the babe, He may fall asleep."

He groaned then looked around. "If we are on the right trail, we
will come to a cave in about half a furlong. I spent the night in
this vicinity a couple times as a youth when we went hunting."

*If, If! What do we do if there is not a cave? What do we do if this is not
the right trail? This seems like a trackless wilderness.*

Fortunately, we were going in the right direction. Yosef could discern
the signs of a path from his vantage better than I could but it took quite
a bit longer than he had expected to find the cave.

Yeshua's cries turned desperate, and lest He work
himself completely out of the baby sling,
Yosef stopped long enough to hand Him to me.
The poor child was much too worked up to settle
down even in my arms. I think, or rather hope,
He was somewhat soothed, knowing that I was cuddling Him
instead of being jostled around on my hard, bowed back. I know
it was a comfort to me as well to be holding Him close.

The stars were brilliant enough so that I could see that the
vegetation was getting scrubbier and more stunted
as we left civilization behind.
From time to time, we saw the faint glint of a lantern in some tiny
hamlet. My heart swelled with pity. Possibly, somebody's Imma
was up tending to the needs of a fretful or feverish child.

Please Adonai, I prayed, may the soldiers be blind to their lights!

I focused on the trail, if it could be called that, once again. We would
have to truly keep our bearings on this rarely traveled shortcut.

I pleaded with Yosef to stop at the cave for the
rest of the night, he uneasily consented.

"They might somehow learn that the baby they were looking
for escaped, and come searching for us," he warned. "It
is too dangerous to make a fire, lest we be seen."

I nodded meekly, but felt chilled to the bone. *How will I ever keep
myself and the little one from freezing to death in this awful cold?*

Yosef unpacked all the blankets and wrapped them snugly
around the baby and me, but he never lay down, not once the
rest of the long frigid night. I dozed off eventually with the
Christ Child snug and as cozy as possible in my arms.

Oh, but my dreams were nightmarish! I would frequently
jerk awake and reach for the baby to see if He was safe.
Each time I looked towards the entry, Yosef was still standing or
sitting near the opening of the cave. It was obvious that he wasn't
going to let anything happen to us if he could possibly help it.

Once, when I opened my eyes, he was kneeling in prayer with a prayer
veil over his head. Behind me, there was deep, scary darkness,
but in front was my husband, guarding us with the help of

the Holy One,
blessed be His Name. It was such a comforting sight that I slept better
after that, in spite of the cold, and the hardness of our 'sanctuary'.

As soon as it was barely light,
Yosef fitted one of the shawls, over my back
so that Yeshua could ride there.

We munched on cheese curds, grapes and flat bread
while traveling. Yeshua seemed contented, though
wide-eyed, according to His earthly father.

Yosef was more relaxed now, he glanced
back occasionally, so we traveled at a leisurely
pace. We were heading towards Egypt.

It would be a long, long trip and so dangerous! The
future loomed ahead, troubled and uncertain.

We traveled by little-used trails for many miles.
Yosef stopped from time to time at lonely sheepfolds or farmhouses
asking for direction. The shepherds were gracious, they shared
their food and accommodations, which really helped.

When we were completely out of the area surrounding Beth Lechem,
we got directions for the well-traveled road next to the Mediterranean
Sea. Now we were able to stop at *khans* during the night..

Tishri 18th

October 4th

DEAR DIARY,

I have not been able to keep the tears from streaming down my face.
My heart aches when I think of the fate of my beloved friends
back in Beth Lechem. How are Ruth and Lydia
coping right at this moment, I wonder?
Are they grieving, or were they somehow spared from
whatever happened? Are any of them yet alive?

I try so hard to put those womanly screams out of my
mind. That terrified sound causes chills to run down
my back. It makes me ill to think of the *aleichem* being
gruesomely murdered, those that I knew and loved.

How narrowly we escaped! How terrified those babies sounded!
I didn't want to think about them but similar thoughts kept
pounding through my brain. How much of Beth Lechem
had been destroyed, or had they surrendered quickly?

Why was quiet little Beth Lechem attacked?
Did it have anything to do with the visit of the Magi so long ago?
I began worrying about the small future King on my back,
I yearned to hold Him close, but could not. It would not be
proper to ask Yosef to stop just so that I could cuddle my babe
in my arms, especially since Yeshua had nodded off to sleep.
I called Yosef to get his attention. He stopped,
turned around, and walked to my side.
"What is it, *Chavivi*?" His face looked haggard
beneath the harsh desert sun.
"Why are they attacking Beth Lechem?" My voice broke.

He slowly stroked Balaam's sweaty neck.
"It came to me in a dream," his shoulders sagged from weariness
and something else I couldn't quite discern. "An angel awoke
me and told me to get up quickly, to take you and the young
one and flee to Egypt, King Herod sought to slay Him."

I dropped my head into my hands and moaned. Instinctively,
I had known they were after the Christ-Child. Feeling
emotionally exhausted, I leaned against his shoulder.

"What is it?"
"What of the others?" I choked out, but could say no more.

He just held me close while I wept. Eventually, we continued
Traveling, but the trail was long and desolate.
We occasionally met a traveler or two but it was a
lonely trek, made lonelier by our great sorrow.

Yosef understood, from what he had read in the prophets, that all the
baby boys would be killed in an effort to destroy the Christ Child.
He was walking ahead in order to lead the donkey,
I was glad.
At least that way he could not see the tears that I was
unable to keep from streaming down my cheeks.
I remember Abba reading from the scroll of Jeremy,
about Rachael weeping for her children, and she would
not be comforted. That must be like now!
I feel so *nephal! (sorry)*

Tishri 20th

October 6th

DEAR DIARY,

Today, we stopped to rest in an oasis beneath palm trees
long before high noon.
Yeshua was glad to get out of the baby carrier, to kick His feet.
Hearing Him gurgle so contentedly caused my eyes to brim with tears
once again. It hurts so to think of dear, sweet little Benoni dead,
as he surely must be.

Oh, Ruth, Ruth. Poor Ruth and Japheth! If my heart is broken
for you, how much worse must you feel? Nay, it is no wonder you
were troubled with such uneasy thoughts back when the wise men
visited our small city! Killing babies, how can men be so wicked?
If I didn't know better, I would think the end of the world was coming.
Yosef had fallen into a sound sleep beneath the slightly cooler
shade of the trees, but I could not. I thought of Lydia, glad
that her little daughter would still be alive, and playing.
I prayed that Lydia would somehow manage to bear
Ruth up in this time of terrible anguish.
I let Yeshua paddle around in a pool of warm water, while supporting
him, of course, and He found it delightfully refreshing. I knew
that later on in the day the water would be much too hot against
His tender skin but was glad that it wasn't yet. Even as I watched
Him splash gleefully, I could scarcely keep from moaning out
loud. I wonder if this ache in my heart will ever go away.

Is this the piercing of the sword that old Shimon *warned me
about that day in the temple? Or will there be more?*

Tishri 21st

October 7th

DEAR DIARY,

I am thinking today about my journey when I went to stay with Aunt
Elisheva. I was so frightened.
So much has happened since then, I feel like I have really changed.
This trip is more dangerous because we are not in a caravan,
while going through the desert, but I feel safer because Yosef
is near me. We both feel a clear sense of *Shekinah*. It feels like
His angels are hovering close by, every step of the way.
We have glimpsed lions and cheetahs in the
distance but they have never come close. Wild dogs come
around a lot, but haven't caused any trouble, except when their
barking keeps us awake at night and wakes the babe.

Tishri 25th

October 11th

DEAR DIARY,

The Red Land, which is how the natives describe the desert, is coming to an end. We can see the pyramids towering in the distance. Tomorrow, we shall enter the Black Land. After well over a week on the run, I am glad to see it.

What will it be like? The people will have strange unfamiliar customs, I am sure. *Will we be accepted? How will we communicate?* It is a truly foreign country, more foreign than Greece even, and so very far from my friends and loved ones.

"Will we be living in Alexandria?" I asked Yosef as we made a little fire over which to roast our parched corn. I had heard that there was a community of our people living there.

Yosef thought for a moment, then shook His head, "It would not be wise. You know how tightly knit our people are. They would naturally wonder why we arrived with little more than the clothes on our backs, rumours would spread."

I nodded. I didn't need him to explain further. Even in Egypt, especially Alexandria, since it was the capital of Egypt, Harod could easily have spies.

Cheshvan 1st

October 17th

DEAR DIARY,

It was a long toilsome journey, but we have finally arrived.
I am resting in a grove of palms near a shady stream
that is trickling towards the *Hapy* River, while Yosef is talking to a
customs officer at the border.
The patrol dog is eying him rather suspiciously, as he is
trained to do. I have never seen a dog with such large black
and white spots before. He looks strange and skinny.
The officer is standing with his arms sternly folded across his
bronzed chest, he seems to have a lot of questions for Yosef.
I got up and stood a little ways behind Yosef.
The dog sniffed at us, then went back to stand guard by his master.
I'm glad the *kelev* didn't get mean because strange dogs frighten me.

The waters of the Hapy River are very swollen.
Oh, I should have called it the Nile.
Hapy is the name of the river god, or something like that, but
Nile is becoming the more common Greek name for it.
I dread the thought of going across in one of those papyrus boats.
Why, they are hardly better than a raft, with their shallow sides.

The customs officer started gesticulating across the river. I wondered
what he was saying and why it must take so long. I suppose the language
barrier is a problem, although he does seem to know some Aramaic.

Yeshua was bouncing excitedly in my arms so I sat on the
grass again. He is just enthralled with all the noisy,
colorful birds that are flying in and out of the rushes. Just imaginethat,
so long ago, a time lost in the mist of the ages, He had a hand in
designing those brilliant pinions, in teaching the birds how to chatter.

Oh, dear, I do hope we won't be turned back! Yosef has turned and is heading our way. He is wiping the sweat off his brow, but his feet aren't dragging so maybe it will be alright.

I'll write more, later.

Because we had the donkey, and too heavy a load for one of those reed fisherman boats, Yosef had to find a spot for us on one of the king's wooden cargo vessels.

I felt the blood drain from my cheeks when I found out how much it would cost, but it didn't take long to cross over, and it did feel much safer than using the reed boats. Good thing we dug under the storage jars before we left.

I am so afraid of crocodiles, I kept searching the waters below us for one of those partly submerged, ugly, leering beasts. I held a certain protesting little man tightly clasped in my arms the whole time. While we were on the near side of the Nile, I thought the village was on a little island, but it is not so. It is actually on a small hill, the flood waters made it appear as an island.

Did our forefathers have to wade through muck like this in order to make their bricks? I wonder how they did it. Did they carry jars of mud to the building site or what?

The first order of the day for Yosef was to find a moneychanger. The captain of the boat would not let me step on dry ground until Yosef had turned the Magi's gift of gold into coins so that he could be paid. I prayed that no robbers would be watching! The next thing we needed to do, of course, was to find a shelter. There was one abandoned house that was crumbling. After the neighbor boys had lost their shyness, they were more than willing,

nay, eager to help smash the worse parts further, a couple of
them even hung around to help us rebuild it.. It felt strange,
finding or asking for straw to mix in with the mud in
order to make the bricks stronger. It felt like history
was repeating itself, almost, but not quite.

I will be most relieved to have a house to live in again, but more than
that, to have these gifts safely stashed away under our dirt floor! That
we will not do 'til well after dark, however. I wonder how long it
will be before we will be safely behind our own walls once again.

DEAR DIARY,

I miss our nice, cool stone cottage in Beth Lechem,
but this will do for a short while.
It is good to have fresh pallets of reeds made and to
rest my weary back on a proper bed once more.
It is also good to be able to let Yeshua crawl all over the hard-
packed dirt floor, without having to worry quite so much
about what he might pick up and put in His mouth.

That reminds me, I will need to get a broom as soon as possible. I
think they are made out of palm branches over here. Maybe I can save
money, and try and make my own. It shouldn't take long.

Yosef is out looking for work. I do not know how he can keep
going. He is so sunburned, so exhausted. Maybe we should have
gone to Alexandria. Surely, our brethren there would have
been quick to find him work.

The last few days have been exhausting, soon after
Yosef left this morning, I crawled onto my pallet and
dozed off with the baby in the circle of my arm.

My sleep was troubled. Maybe it was because of a vanished dream,
but when I awoke, I was worried about my companions back in
Beth Lechem. My heart weeps for them, but at the same time I am
concerned about our own future. Will we be accepted, here? Will we
find other Hebrew children with whom we can fellowship? Above all,
will Yosef be able to find work? Oh *El Shaddai*, help us to trust in You,
and commit the future into Your keeping. Things look so bleak.

12th Chisleu

November 26th

DEAR DIARY,

It is pleasant to wake up to the sounds of singing and laughter
each morning. I have watched dozens of farm workers tramp
by on their way to fields which they have to irrigate every day.
If Yosef wasn't a carpenter, I think he would gladly join
the workers in the fields. I know I would if I was a man
and if they didn't speak such a fast gibberish!

I find it fascinating, watching a crew harvesting papyrus reeds
just a short walk from where we live. It is amazing, seeing them
haul six to eight-foot bundles on their lithe young bodies.
When I saw some of them nibble at the tips, I tried it
too; it was actually quite sweet, delectable! I took some
home for a snack, it had fallen during transport

Marilyn Friesen

8th Tevet

December 21st

DEAR DIARY,

I am running really low on parchment. I wonder if it would be at all
possible to make some papyrus. It looks complicated,
but I would like to try.

10th Tevet

December 23rd

DEAR DIARY,

My face is flaming with embarrassment. I went to watch the papyrus
workers today, then I saw that some of them had no clothes on!
I turned and crept away, but the shame lingers with me still.
Obviously, I will have to find something else to do to fill my days

12th Tevet

December 25th

DEAR DIARY,

Oh, Holy *Adonai*; hallowed be Thy Name, help me not to complain like the children of Yisrael did so long ago. I am finding it so hard to dwell in this hot dry foreign land!

I am lonesome for my naughty little goat; I miss the five colorful chickens and the one cock. Our chicks would have hatched out long ago. Who would care for them? I hate to think of them starving to death or being stolen away by a *nesher* or some other birds of prey!

I long to see our cottage and work in our tiny garden once more. My plants would be getting to be such a nice size by now, if the weeds have not choked them out!

But most of all, I miss my friends! Every time I think of Ruthalei, I feel like crying my eyes out. I can't get the awful picture out of my mind's-eye, the sharp, flashing sword lunging at her tiny boy, probably, she clung to him with terror in her eyes. How could the soldiers do that? Are they not abbas? At least some of them!

Oh Benoni, Benoni, my heart is broken for you! What a terrible way to die. There now, I just took a deep breath. Even though my hand is still shaking, I will try to write of more cheerful things.

I am sure Benoni's guardian angel snatched him swiftly away, up to Heaven. But do not you think he misses his mother just a little bit, even up there in Paradise? After all, he was such a little boy!

I think I will be able to convince myself that Benoni is fine now, but oh, my heart bleeds for Ruth, Japheth, and the many other parents. If I remember correctly, there was at least twenty-five little boys under the age of two living in our neighborhood!

Just now, Yosef walked in, and I asked him about our place in Beth Lechem. He said that soon after we arrived, he sent a message with a caravan, to ask Jose and Esther to care for it until we come back. I am sure they will not mind, since they were looking for a place to rent for their soon-to-be-married children. People must have been amazed when we disappeared so suddenly and completely! I'm curious to know what they said to each other.

17th Shebat

January 28th

DEAR DIARY,

I have been waking up every hour or more with this hacking cough. Nothing seems to help, and sometimes I feel like I will choke when I cough so hard. What can I do, what can I take to relieve the misery?

I wonder if it is something in this foreign air that makes me cough.

Last night I crept silently out of bed in an effort to not
disturb Yosef, and peered out of the window.
Even at night the dimly formed outlines seem unfamiliar. I can
see our small cluster of adobe brick houses huddled on the banks
of the gleaming Nile, and there are palm trees here and there.

Nothing is cozy and home-like. Even the fishy smell that hovers faintly
in the air reminds me that this is not our Navara or Beth Lechem.
My friends and family seem far away, tears formed in my eyes, but
then I started violently coughing once again. No time for tears.

I am so lonesome for Imma, Hanalei and all the rest. I tried to pray for
Lydia and Ruth but it is quite useless when my head is pounding so.
I would lay back down but that only makes the coughing worse.

Oh, Adonai, I cried inwardly, *Have mercy on me. I have
been sick now for two weeks. When will I get better?*
Oh, that we had never been torn away from
our beloved family in Navara!
Baby Yeshua is not feeling well either,
so we keep each other company at night.
He is miserable because of His own nasty fever, and loose stools, besides
cutting teeth. The poor darling . . . I know of few ways to comfort him.

Later, Yosef brought me some catnip. Hopefully that will help relieve my cough. I made a tea with it. I also stirred some cloves into wild honey like mother used to do. Tonight I will strain off the cloves, and take a spoonful of the concoction when a coughing spell strikes. Perhaps, between the two remedies, I will be able to get some sleep!

I asked Yosef permission to let the housework slide a little because the baby is ill and I feel so unwell.

He nodded and put his arm around my shoulder.

24th Shebat

February 4th

DEAR DIARY,

I feel so much more invigorated now that I am over my cough. It lasted for nearly three long weeks, and I hope to never ever go through something like that again! Yeshua is not sick anymore either, so do I rejoice? Yes!

I went for a walk down to the river this morning
with the baby straddled over my hip.

It felt strange looking down at the very same waters that rocked *Mosheh* to sleep in his little reed basket all those many centuries ago. I am so glad it wasn't me that had to entrust my infant to the flowing river.

What if some horrible old crocodile had been lurking nearby? *Jochabed* was so brave, but when a mother is desperate she will do almost anything to save her *chavivi*. I am sure, though, that she must have worried about leaving her baby to the mercies of . . . who knows what.

If it would have been me, I would have searched for the
thickest, sturdiest clump of reeds ever, so that the cradle
would not drift one handbreadth down the river.

Although *Mosheh's* mother must have been deeply
concerned about leaving her small son there,
do you not think the baby would have found it lovely and relaxing
to drift off to sleep with the sunlight delicately penetrating
the woven basket cover while the *boat* rocked gently?

I wonder if his mother knew that the princess was a kind-
hearted woman that often went there to bathe.

Our forefathers have been on my mind a lot lately.
I've strolled around the towering pyramids on more than one
occasion, they remind me of how hard our ancestors had to labor to
gather straw and make bricks for all these huge building projects.
How did they ever move those stones?
Were people more intelligent, taller and stronger, than
they are now? Those pyramids are really incredible.

27ᵗʰ Shebat

February 7ᵗʰ

DEAR DIARY,

Yosef read what I wrote when I was feeling sick and lonely.
To my surprise, he did not admonish me but turned
to hurry out of our arched doorway.
He called over his shoulder that he would be back soon.
Naturally, I was quite mystified, I watched as
he strode briskly down the street.

When he turned a corner, I lost sight of him, so I went
back to preparing the fish and vegetables for supper.
Soon he was back with a guest whom he identified as a
basket maker. The elderly man was carrying a short bundle
of the outer rinds of papyrus stalks in his arms.

"You have wished to learn how to make papyrus," Yosef
explained, "So I have asked an acquaintance to teach you
how to make a reed mat, you can go on from there."

I was surprised that Yosef would allow me to have a heathen
man for my teacher, but perhaps he thought it was permissible
because he would always be here during lessons.
Besides, he never did feel it was right to shun
the Gentiles as rigidly as some would.

I'm sure my eyes were sparkling with joy.
Yeshua wouldn't get nearly so grubby if I could
make a few mats to scatter across the floor.
After that, I would like to tackle baskets,
and maybe even papyrus.
It is very expensive to buy papyrus, but I can't bear the thought of
not being to write my thoughts down whenever the urge strikes me!

I wish to say that we ate quickly so that I could hurry on with my lesson, but that is not Yosef's way. After our leisurely repast, during which our guest taught us many words for common everyday objects, and greetings, I cleared away the meal and washed the dishes.

Trei-Vaj-Hoiden laid out the reeds in preparation for the
first lesson. *Yeshua* was so eager to crawl all over the reeds
that Yosef scooped Him up and held Him in his arms.
Making a mat wasn't hard at all! It was fun, actually,
and I think I will even figure out how to weave
a design into the border of the next
one I am planning to do.

29th Adar

March 11th

DEAR DIARY,

Sorry, Imma, I haven't written for several weeks because I have been so
busy. I hope you have received my scrolls from time to time.
Thank you for every single one you have written. I read
them over and over then tuck them safely in our chest.

My first basket was a clumsy looking affair,
the second, not much better, but the third one I am not ashamed
to take with me shopping next time I go. I'll use the other ones for
Yeshua's dirty laundry . . . or something. Actually, one of them will
be fine for picking up things around the house and returning them
to where they belong since I don't need it for gardening this year.

Lately, I have been working on my finest project of all… Papyrus!

Trei-Vaj-Hoiden helped me to get the papyrus strips cut thin enough,
then lay them at right angles to each other on a piece of linen.
He moistened them the first time to get just the right amount
of water on them, then I added another layer of linen.
I had to pound for a long time to get the sap to
seep out, and stick all those strips together.
After it had dried, it was so exciting to hold up my
very first piece of homemade papyrus.

Yosef shared in my joy; Trei-Vaj-Hoiden's dark, craggy face was wreathed
in smiles, even Yeshua clapped His pudgy little hand. Trei-Vaj-Hoiden
is such a nice elderly man… I wish he would become a proselyte.

I was eager to start on another sheet,
but Yosef reminded me that it was time to go to bed.
I could see that the men were exhausted from the long day
of work so quietly, albeit unenthusiastically, submitted.

24th Nisan

April 4th

DEAR DIARY,

What a neglected scroll, even though I have all those wonderful fresh
new pieces of papyrus piling up.
Today I am going to glue them together with resin and roll
them into one long scroll. I can hardly wait until this parchment
is finished so I can start on the lovely brand new scroll.

Trei-Vaj-Hoiden is impressed with how fast and neat I have
become. He says he has never had a worker that
learned to do such a good job
so quickly.
I think it is because I am eager to have plenty on hand.
He hasn't asked why we want so much papyrus,
I don't think he would believe it if I told him I knew how to write.

Of course I can't write in Egyptian (*Medounetcher*). They have
seven hundred different symbols or pictures to learn, I am not
about to tackle that! Aramaic or Hebrew, is fine for me.

If Yosef allows me,
I am thinking of making and selling baskets and mats
in exchange for food and other things at the market. They are
so easy and quick to do and I enjoy working with my hands.
It would be fun to have a stall in the village,
I think I now know enough of the language to get by.

18th Iyyar

April 28th

DEAR DIARY,

Making baskets and mats has been occupying much of my spare time
and they sell readily. Possibly the main reason my products sell
so quickly is because Yeshua is always with me, He is so cheery and
personable that the women, and even some of the men are attracted
to my stall because of Him. They are delighted with how He greets
them in their language and waves his pudgy hands so cheerfully.

I feel good about the sales because we don't have to dip
into *Yeshua's gift money* so much now. He will surely need
it when He sets up His kingdom, will he not?

I actually have more free time here than I did in Yisrael since
I do not have to go down to the river to wash the clothes.
Here that is not considered work for *aant'at*s to do.
With crocodiles and hippopotamus lurking nearby,
it is safer for the men to do the washing.
What a relief, but how unfamiliar at the same time.
I hope I won't be thoroughly
spoiled by the time we get back to Judea.

I do miss having a garden of my own but last week I was glad
we didn't have one. I felt so sorry for some of our *aleichem*
because much of their freshly sprouted crop had been destroyed by
a hippopotamus. They will be able to replant, but what a setback.

I brought the *aleichem* that live nearby
a little fresh bread in a basket, they seemed to appreciate it. I am
intrigued with how many different kinds of breads these villagers
know how to bake but I get hungry for the kind we made at home.

21st Iyyar

May 1st

DEAR DIARY,

Someone stopped by a while ago.
I wished so much that it would be a new Jewish friend!
We appreciate *Trei-Vaj-Hoiden* because he is so unpretentious, but
he is an old man. I do not care to call him a heathen, although
that is what he is. Please, *El'Elohim,* may there be a place in
Paradise for such neighbourly people.

If we had moved to Alexandria, I might have had many friends
by now. I wonder if Yosef would ever reconsider moving there.
A dear little *talitha* was standing at the door
with a kitten dangling in her hands. I could not understand
a word she said but her body language was clear.
She obviously wanted me to have the kitten, now I am the uncertain
owner of a four-legged creature who wants to be in the house with us.

I do hope that Yosef will not mind.
Yeshua loves it so. We have never had a cat before but I hear
they are supposed to be skillful at catching rodents.

DEAR DIARY,

Yosef was appalled when he saw the cat.
"Mary'am," he exclaimed, "why did you allow
that filthy creature in the house?"
"But it's only a kitten, and Yeshua loves it, so," I stammered.
"A kitten, Mary'am; it's a cat! Know you not
that the heathen worship these things?
Bastet is their cat goddess! What were you ever thinking?"
"I, I don't know."
Tears sprang into my eyes so I turned away.
Yosef picked it up gingerly by the scuff of the neck
and carried it out.

When Yeshua realized His small plaything had been taken away,
He howled loudly.
I was trying to comfort Him when Yosef returned.

He stood in the doorway and stared at us for a moment.
I looked away and tried to discreetly wipe my own
tears with the corner of my head covering.
He came over and took Yeshua from me but
his eyes were averted.
"Mary'am, I didn't mean to make you cry."
Yeshua squirmed to get down so Yosef tossed
Him up in the air until He giggled.
It wasn't quite so easy for me to feel happy.
"It's just that we are HaShem"s Chosen People.
We must keep ourselves separate from the sinners. How
would it look if a practicing Jew owned a cat?"
I shrugged my shoulders.
"Are you pouting?"

I looked up, feeling a bit frightened.
"I'm sorry, Yosef, but *Yeshua* likes it so much."
And I did to.

Yosef sighed and held the baby above his head again.
He looked at me uncertainly then placed Yeshua on
the reed mat at his feet before walking out.

28th Iyyar

May 8th

DEAR DIARY,

What a cruel world we live in! Originally, we had heard that all baby boys two-years-old and under had been killed in Beth Lechem, but today a traveler told us what really happened.

All the babies all of them, two-years-old and under were slaughtered! Of course I should have assumed as much because little girls are dressed exactly the same as the boys at that age. But why would innocent toddlers have to be the victims of some horrible political scheme? Has such an awful thing ever happened before? They're mere babies!

It has been hours since the news arrived, yet I am still too numbed with shock to even cry. When I first heard the awful news, I felt an urgent need to hold our baby so I clung to Him while my tears soaked His hair. I stared at nothing in particular while our *chavivi tinoki*, (beloved little child), wrapped His arms around my neck, Yosef held both of us.

29th Iyyar

May 9th

DEAR DIARY,

I wrote a letter to be shared with all those I met with at the well, who are now in mourning. My heart sorrows for them, although it does help a little to send off that script.

A caravan of fine linen and other goods is
leaving for *Yerushalayim* today. Yosef gave instructions to one of the
merchants to have the letter delivered to my dohd Zachariah,
a well-known priest.
Zachariah will gladly see to it that the letter reaches Beth Lechem,
which is only a few furlongs away from *Yerushalayim*.

I can just about see the smile on his face when he recognizes my
handwriting. It will bring back memories of the many happy
hours we spent on the stone bench beside the sundial.
Actually, I wasn't often sitting on the bench but kneeling in
front of it in order to use it for my table.
You probably remember that I was so interested in
reading the Torah for myself that he taught me
how to read and write.

Oh, how can I write about such mundane things
when my friends have lost their...BABIES!

Sivan 1

May 10th

DEAR DIARY,

I have been having thoughts about *HaShem*, hallowed be His Name, that I am too shy to share even with Yosef. *Adonai* is so high and holy that He often seems almost unapproachable by us, mere mortals. Isn't that thick heavy veil in the temple meant to symbolize our separation from Him?

But when I look at Yeshua, my delightful little *tinoki,* and remember that *El'Shaddai,* which means Savior, is His Father, I wonder if there is a side to *HaShem* that is more approachable.

Sometimes, I have even dared to address Him as my Father, only in my mind of course. Perhaps only the holy men like the prophets, were allowed to address him thus, but His *Shekinah* seems so close and comforting when I do.

This even-tide, I found this, it's near the beginning of the Torah.

And behold I am with thee,
And will keep thee in all places
Whither thou goest,
and will bring thee again into this land;
For I will not leave thee,
until I have done that which I have spoken
to thee of.

Now, that's a promise I want to cling to while
I am so far from home

Sivan 5

May 14th

DEAR DIARY,

We never actually allow that kitten into the house,
but she keeps coming around. I marvel at how gentle
Yeshua is with it.
He waves His tiny hands and trills with joy whenever the little thing
patter-pats near Him. Of course whenever I see them together,
I remove our little boy. It is hard for me to believe that
something so sweet and cuddly would be wrong to own
but I must submit to the teachings of the *rebbe*.

Sivan 7th

May 16th

DEAR DIARY,

Praise *Yahweh*! I have met another Yisraelite. We have so little in common that it is almost ludicrous. *Astral's* family has lived in Egypt for many generations. They are descendants of the mixed multitude that trailed after Moshe into the wilderness, but then returned to Egypt. I am still very lonely for my homeland but at least I have someone to talk to now, even though her accent is hard to understand. Astral is the grandmother of the little *riba* who gave us the kitten.

I often wonder how my friends and family are doing.

We have not heard from anyone for a long time,

I am so lonely.

4ᵗʰ Tammuz

June 12ᵗʰ

DEAR DIARY,

Praise Jehovah ! I got a letter today. I was so happy, I felt I could sail to the stars like the angels! It was from Ruth, of all people. Dear sweet Ruthalei thought about me in spite of all her own troubles. She is a true friend. I will insert it here, just for the record. You will find it amusing, how literally her brother wrote down *everything* she said.

Dear Miry'am 27th Iyyr

With eagerness I hastened off to find my elder brother who is a scribe,
the moment my duties were done this evening!
Shalom my dearest friend! What occupies your time way off there
in the land of Egypt? Besides the normal, you know.
Do you have a garden? Our gan (gardens) are doing great this year.
I know it's silly, but Lydia and I are having a competition to see who
can harvest the most cucumbers! It's fun!
My brother is telling me to get down to business, and avoid all this
idle talk. (And he actually wrote that!)
Imma stayed with me in at the beginning of the rainy season. I
do not see my Imma as much since she moved to Yerushalayim after
remarrying. It was such a comfort to have her around. I did not know
what to think, let alone how to respond, when she said she was betrothed
to Abner, the brick layer. I know Abner is a respected gentleman, and
has been a widower for many years, but I can't imagine anyone taking
Abba's place, even though it is going on two years since he was struck
by lightening while winnowing wheat.
I have some very special news to share with you. The beginning
of the New Year will have special meaning for us this fall. We will
be having another little one around the time of Rosh Hashanah, but
probably before the Day of Atonement.
He or she can never take the place of our dear *Benoni*, but we are
comforted to know that Benoni is safe with the angels.
When are you coming home? We all miss you so much. I do not
think a week passes without someone bringing up your name, and
wondering how you are all keeping. Thank you so much for that letter
you sent . . . after, well you know what.

Zachariah's cousin brought it to our early morning meeting place
at the well, and someone hastened off to ask the Rabboni if he would
read it for us. While Rabboni Nathan bar Solomon read, some of us
clung to each other, and wept. Don't worry, there were happy tears
mingled with the sorrowing ones. We were just so gad for your sweet
words of comfort.

Remember **Haghaar**? I do not know if you can believe this, but she
is not nearly so bristly lately! I think it touched her heart what some of
us mothers have had to go through.

Actually the whole town was in mourning.

There are a lot of bitter words spoken against the King, and I am
afraid no tears are being lost over the reports that he is dreadfully sick,
possibly dying. One does wonder about his poor soul, though.

Give your little *riba* a big hug and a kiss from me. I guess he is not
so very little any more. He must be running all over the place by now,
and prattling away like everything. How sweet!

I must stop! My brother is scowling, and muttering about how
aant'at always talks too much!" Yet he wrote that, also!

"I miss you! Please write soon!

Much love,

Ruth

Did you smile at those comments about Ruth's brother?
Everyone knows he has a soft spot in his heart for Ruth.
I rejoice for the woman whom he soon will marry.

6th Tammuz

June 14th

DEAR DIARY,

Yosef flexed his arms and placed the lantern
at the center of the table.
A silver crescent of a moon peered in the window.
I was sitting on a sleeping bench nearby, enjoying
his presence while rocking the baby.

"Well, that ebony chest got done in plenty of time for Lo-Jonj-Ammi's
wedding," Yosef directed one of his rare but winning smiles at me.
"I did the finishing touches just before supper, Mazel-
can—tcejbo can pick it up in the morning."

He sighed, I looked up quickly. "What troubles you, my *Chavivi*?"
Yeshua stirred at the sound of my voice and opened His eyes,
so I pulled the blanket partly over His cheek and
resumed humming.

"It's those Egyptian symbols that Mazel-can—tcejbo insisted
that I carve around the edge of the lid and chest."

Yosef leaned back with his head resting on his folded hands.
"He claims they are meaningless, but I am not so sure. Why
would he want them carved there if they were meaningless?

"I was told they signify good fortune, long life and happiness.
Would *HaShem*, hallowed be His Name, truly be pleased
with them? Will He be pleased with me for engraving
them? Of course Mazel-can—tcejbo is an Egyptian."

"Oh, to be back in our own country,

Marilyn Friesen

among our own people," I murmured, rocking my *tinoki* gently.
There we would not have to rub shoulders with all these foreigners.
I pressed *Yeshua's* head against my heart. Yeshua is also getting
acquainted with the Egyptian way of doing things,
I do not know how detrimental the influence might be.
He can jabber as many words in the Egyptian
language as He can in Aramaic.

On the other hand, although He is still very little,
and bigger children take advantage of Him by snatching things
away from Him, I have never once seen Him throw Himself
on the ground in a fit of temper. That is truly noteworthy
because it is not that He is a timid little fellow.

One thing that has moistened my eyes more than once
is seeing Him offer a plaything to another *riba*.
He seems so tiny to understand the concept of sharing.
I am tempted to hover over Him lest other children get
too rough, but I must know when to restrain myself.

Yosef recalled a verse in the Holy Writ about "out of Egypt have I called
my Son." Surely that must be referring to this sweet *tinoki* that I take
so much pleasure in caring for. If so long ago, it was predicted that
He would live here for a time, surely He will protect our little boy.

Early last evening, a tiny boy, even smaller than our Yeshua,
fell and scraped his knee. He was howling buckets
and Yeshua bent over to give him *oh-oh*. Just then his
mother came and roughly snatched up her boy.

She glared at Yeshua, saying, "Did you push him?" Yeshua just
stood there looking up at her with His beautiful clear green eyes,
and solemnly shook His head. I could not hear His reply;
I was hovering just inside the window, but
the woman shrugged her
shoulders scornfully and strode back into the house.

Today, the two little fellows are playing happily once again.
Yosef is sitting near me at the table while I write.
His head keeps nodding, then he jerks awake. Poor man, he
is so tired. I wish he would just go to bed, but it is still early
and I suppose he's afraid someone might come over.

Something at the window seems strange, so I will
lay aside my papyrus and pen to investigate.

Remember that little old lady I told you about? I do want to
be kind, but she turned out to be, well, different. We had not
closed our shutters tonight in order to let in fresh air.

Well, before I got to the wind-hole, she poked her
head inside, and in her shrill voice, she called,

"Yosef!"

The poor, dear sleepy man nearly jumped out of his skin! With
her long hooked nose and straggly black hair, she does give one a
start. Although she is of Yisraelite decent, she has more heathen
ways than many of our Egyptian *Aleichem* (neighbors).

She thrust a hissing black cat through the window and asked
us if we wanted it. She has five or six cats of her own, this
stray tom was always coming over and causing a ruckus.

Yosef politely declined. Didn't she know we had already cast one out?
Although we never feed the kitten, she keeps coming around.
When I see Yeshua playing with it, I take Him away, but
likely there are many times I don't see them together.

I wonder what our *aleichem* think of a little Jewish boy lugging
a cat around. Perhaps, they are quite pleased? Incidentally, this
feisty creature that we were offered has markings, in three different
colors, which is quite unusual. Surely it is highly revered.

DEAR DIARY,

I am having trouble sleeping tonight mainly because of the incessant heat, and the annoying gnats. Maybe I'll try rubbing spearmint on my face and arms if I ever find some in the market. Astral insists it will keep the insects away.

A lantern is by my side, I am trying to
catch a breath of fresh air on our roof top. It is not a quiet night.
A cat is prowling down the alley, I think it just met up
with another one that must have invaded its territory,
a terrible hissing, spitting, and yowling has resulted.

Now on the housetop, I can see another cat
tiptoeing archly around the ledge, I watched as it paused to
listen to the furious duet. Now the brawlers have been joined
by several more vagabonds, the din is most eerie
sounding, and to think I came up here to rest!

There is some sort of royal dignitary who lives on the top of
the hill to the west of us. He must have forgotten to
tie up his tall, skinny half-grown pups because all
three of them are tearing down the street just now,
tails wagging, while yapping in high glee.

You should have seen those felines scatter!
To be sure, one or two of them put on a momentary show
of bravado but it did not last. After one hissing tom got
shook between the teeth by an exuberant pup,
the others decided they had more pressing matters to attend to.

I can hear Prince Tirades-de-Yele shouting at the trio and I
see several *aleichem* peering out of windows and doors.
It doesn't take much to imagine the heavy scowls lining their jowls.

Just for the record, yea, I did duck from view before anyone could
see me. It would hardly be fitting for a matronly young *aant'at*
like myself to be seen hanging over the rooftop when the
Prince is galloping down the street at midnight.
Oh dear, all that commotion, or was it the sudden
silence that followed, has awakened my little boy.
I must hasten to his side lest he grow frightened and
awaken His dear tired Abba.

22nd Elul

September 9th

DEAR DIARY,

We received news from our homeland today. King Herod is dead so now it is safe to go back. Apparently, he died quite suddenly. I am so happy, happy, happy! Not happy that he died of course, but they we can return. I can hardly contain myself. I can hardly wait to see Lydia, Ruth, and all the rest.

25th Elul

September 12th;

DEAR DIARY,

There nights have passed, once again I am doing my writing with a
lamp by my side. I am not sure what awakened me this time.
Yosef and I were debating long after darkness fell
about where we should move to in Judea.

I yearn to go to Beth Lechem where we were given such a
warm welcome. I can't find words to express my desire,
yea, it is almost a need, to hug my friends and
comfort them after their devastating grief.

Yosef thinks they will have moved on with their lives by now; but if
you lose a darling *tinoki,* the pain gets wedged deep into the heart,
and it never completely eases, isn't that so?

If we don't move back to Beth Lechem, will I ever see my friends
again? Oh, I shouldn't have such a dark view of things.

We will surely go to the Passover as often as possible, I can meet my
friends there. If not, perhaps we can spend a day in Beth Lechem
after the Passover. It is only a few furlongs from Yerushalayim.

My *chavivi* fears for our Son's safety if we return to Beth Lechem. Of
course I share his concern. It is so close to *Yerushalayim.* It has been
reported that a son of Herod is on the throne and he is considered just as
untrustworthy as his sire. Of course, Yeshua's safety has absolute priority.

As I have shared before, caring for the divine
Son of El Elohim is an awesome responsibility! It is a challenge
trying to figure out what is best for Him. In so many ways,

He is much like other boys, but *we* know who He is and *we*
have been entrusted with the duty of guiding Him.

Will it make much of a difference where He is raised? Is an obscure
village good enough? Will it make it harder for him to adjust to
His calling as an adult if we make too many mistakes as parents?

My feelings about going back to Navara are mixed.
My heart leaps with joy and anticipation at the thought of
seeing Imma and the younger children once again,
but Abba, dear stern Abba was so disapproving when we
left to wend our way over the hills and the valleys,
heading to Beth Lechem just before the babe came into the world.
He actually turned his back on me and refused to say farewell.
My heartache was so great because I felt he had
practically disowned me! I just thought of
it now; maybe he just didn't know how to respond to me.
Maybe he was even hiding tears—oh, wistful thought!

Yosef feels it would be safer to raise Yeshua
in a remote place like Navara. He is so wise that I yearn to trust
him completely in this matter, but something within me hesitates.

What will I do if Yeshua is shunned in our home town? I asked
Yosef if he thought He would receive the opportunities there to be
groomed for His future role as King? We talked soberly about it
for a long while.

All the direction we perceived was for the present, with trembling
hands we must commit the future into the hands of *Adonai*.
Oh, so often I need to entreat the Lord El Elohim to guide
us so we will do what is right with our precious charge.

4th Tishri

September 20th

DEAR DIARY,

I am reminiscing today about our last morning in Egypt. The reaction
to our leaving was most unexpected.
All the children from our neighborhood gathered at our
house while we were finishing up the packing.
Several of the half-grown youngsters wanted to lug
Yeshua around. He did not like that very much,
He is quite capable of scampering around on His own sturdy
little legs. Twice, I heard Him say, "Put me down, please,"
but I was too busy packing to see if they complied.

We are traveling with a caravan, which I suppose will be much safer
than the way we scurried through the desert on our way here.
Today, I had the rare scary opportunity to ride on the back of a camel.
The ground seemed very far down, but the view was incredible.
The best part of the ride was how shaded Yeshua and I were from the
burning sun because of the large green canopy over our heads. I felt
quite safe and comfortable once I was safely settled into the-box-like
carrier on the camel's back. Actually, I felt like a foreign princess!

The merchant who owns the camel has taken a liking to our little lad.
I suppose I got to ride mostly for Yeshua's sake,
in order to keep Him company.
Tomorrow, I will be bumping along on the donkey's back as usual,
and promise not to complain.

Yosef purchased an expensive ointment before we left to
prevent our *tinoki*"s delicate skin from burning.
He has encouraged me to faithfully use it also.
What a relief not to have a blistered nose or
cheeks, forehead, and all the rest!

I'm blushing as I write. I had asked Yosef if it would be
alright to use the black makeup, *kohl*, around my eyes. It
is not only for beauty, it would also protect my eyes from
infection and dust while crossing the Red Land.

But Yosef shook his head, nay. "Learn not the way of the
heathen," he admonished. "I will buy you a fine thin veil of
the best Egyptian linen. That will help much, yes?"

Now, when I think it over, I feel ashamed for even mentioning
it. I would have appeared so strange, so barbaric,
with that thick stuff on my face.

We shopped for the linen veil in a leisurely manner, although
I suspect Yosef was not particularly enthused about
lingering at the market as I was.
I am very happy with the veil we purchased.
It will be a wonderful memory of our sojourn in Egypt.
It doesn't have graven images embroidered on it,
which is forbidden, but has a graceful
design in gold with green accents, very attractive it

5th Tishri

September 21st

DEAR DIARY,

Do you remember me telling you about that child who fell and hurt himself a while ago? Just before Yosef hoisted our little boy in front of me on the donkey, his mother hurried out, pulling her toddler by the hand, and told *Reia-bek-tnafni-keihn* to say goodbye to Yeshua.

I was surprised, yes, but what amazed me even more was that she twirled some of Yeshua's soft dark curls around her fingers and said; "You are such a sweet boy. We will miss you."

I will chat with her again in Paradise, yes? Oh, I do hope so!

Yeshua has a way of looking at people in such a sweetly solemn way. This He did before impulsively hugging His little friend. I wonder how much He understands about us going away.

7th Tishri

September 23rd

DEAR DIARY,

The most appalling sandstorm came up very swiftly. We could not see anything, so naturally we could not go anywhere after the sand started blowing. I wrapped my mantle around Yeshua,
I held him close, but got the feeling
I was more afraid than He was. He was so quiet, and soon I realized He must be listening to the wind, so I tried to quiet my erratically beating heart, to listen also. I was not as enthralled with the weird lonely sound of the wind tearing through the desert sands as He appeared to be!

I guess Yeshua knew I wasn't enjoying it because He wrapped His arms around me and whispered,
"All is well, Imma. It will soon be over."

Yosef groped around until he found a lamp and managed to get it lit in order to set up the tent. For an instant, we glimpsed the other camels, donkeys and fellow travelers huddled around, but soon the light was snuffed out by the wind.

There was something comforting about getting a second chance to see the others huddled close by.
Yosef and I sort of leaned into each other inside our black goat hair tent, which is difficult to set up under the best of circumstances and virtually impossible now. We shouldn't have tried. The wind whipped it off of us and it went flying away across the desert.

Our faces were almost totally covered with our mantles
but my eyes stung anyway, I kept crunching grit between my
teeth. Yeshua fell asleep in my arms so Yosef took Him
and we let Him snuggle across both our laps.

I had no idea what time it was by then, but the storm had
struck shortly after high noon. We finally rolled ourselves up
in our bedding, gritty though it was, and tried to sleep,
since the wind was showing no signs of letting up. I was finding it
very difficult to breathe, that always makes me feel so panicky.
Poor Yeshua, He is so tiny to have to endure
such dreadful weather conditions!

We must have eventually been lulled to sleep because
the next thing I heard made me feel chilled.
One of the guides had accidentally let it slip that they were
inexperienced, this was their first time guiding alone. I soon pitied
them, however, when I heard the merchants curse and rage at them.

When I saw the caravan master shaking his fist under
the young escort's nose, his glowering partners
standing around with their arms crossed,
I ducked my head under the covers until it felt safer to come out.

When I did, I saw plenty of activity all around,
including Yosef feeding the donkey from a nosebag.
Although the moon was high in the sky,
I realized we would soon be traveling. Yeshua barely awakened
when Yosef set him in front of me on the donkey.
He wrapped His arms and
legs around me, rested His dark curly head against my bosom,
and was soon fast asleep again as we plodded along.
My dear *tinoki,* what
a love.

When we stopped for breakfast, a small slave boy innocently asked if
we hadn't been very near to a den of extremely poisonous vicious
vipers when the dust storm struck.
The guides vehemently denied it of course,
but later I heard the desperate, anguished screams of the little
riba. I prayed, with tears trickling down my face, that they
would please, please stop striking him.
Finally, they did.

No doubt there would have been wide-spread panic if
vipers had been discovered nearby, but oh, I do wish
that little boy had kept his mouth shut and not gotten
himself into so much trouble.
It must have been terrifying for the Children of Yisrael when they
were wandering in this very desert, many were smitten by serpents.

DEAR DIARY,

We are back in Navara now, I will record a conversation I overheard at the synagogue this morning. You may judge for yourself how I feel about it.

"So … Mary'am *Yosef bar Yaakov* has returned to Navara! They were gone so long, I thought she would never dare to show herself in these parts again! It's quite stubborn of Yosef to insist, I must add."

"What in the entire Roman kingdom are you talking about," a younger voice demanded.

"Oh? Do not you recall? There was something suspicious about the birth of that boy of hers."
"Suspicious? Whatever do you mean?
You are talking barbaric to me!"

"Think . . . Are you not thinking?
You do simple arithmetic, no? Everyone knows that Yosef is not the father. Was he even home at the time?"
There was a long silence.

"Oh," the other voice said and he slunk away.

My cheeks burned as if in shame, even though
I had done nothing wrong.
How am I ever going to deal with the stares, the snide remarks of the self-righteous?
I worried.

Yeshua reached up to take my hand and looked at me

with a wide questioning gaze,
but did not say anything. I am so glad He is
too young to understand . . . so far!
How can I bear to look into His pure innocent eyes
and see the hurt that will eventually come if He hears some evil-
minded people imply that I must be little better than a *zonah*.
That is another way of calling someone a—harlot! It will hurt
worse yet, when He learns the meaning of the word illegitimate!

If Yosef was His father, it would have been considered somewhat more
forgivable, but since His fatherhood is supposedly unknown, stories will
linger . . . What pains me deeply is that I can't be around to protect
Him from all the unjust accusations that may be hurled at Him!
And yet at the same time I do feel so unworthy,
too unholy to carry the sacred Son of God. It is the cry
of my heart to be more pure within; more holy, more…
worthy to be the mother of such a Holy Child.

And yet illegitimate is what He is being called. What an ugly word!
Oh, the pain it brings to countless numbers of blameless children.
It is not their sin that caused them to be born, but
they must suffer the scorn and reproach!

Tzedakah comes to mind, just now.
She was one of the wenches who frequently came to
beg for a morsel of bread when I was a child.
Most of the children would hurl stones, chase her away.
Oh, the words they would shout at her were
so terrible, but the adults didn't care.
I remember sitting in the open door of our house with
my hands on my chin, sorrowfully watching her.
Although our mother was kind,
even she had instructed us not to play with her.
That word had been whispered about her.
Imma slipped her food when she thought no one was looking.

Ironically, her name means *mercy; deeds of kindness*.
I know now that her mother was pleading with
us to be kind to her by naming her thus.

Then, there are the Elias twins.
I do not even recall their names. The last I'd heard, they were living a
rough life as pirates. They were always fighting, using foul language.
If we had not ostracized them so badly,
would they have acted differently?

I wonder if the mothers of these children are still living.
Were they stoned? Our parents never allowed us to be on the
streets when something like that was about to happen;
they certainly wouldn't talk about it in our presence.

While at the synagogue today, I saw *Tzedakah* huddled
in a corner of the outer court, so smiled at her.
Her eyes widened in surprise but she did not return my
smile. Next Shabbat, I would like to sit next to her, or
will that just make matters worse?

Maybe the so-called righteous ones will say that this proves
I am sinful woman. How could I have forgotten?
it is not even allowed for her to go beyond the outer court.

As I led Yeshua to a seat in the *aant'ats* balcony, it seemed like every head
pivoted towards us, yet there were no smiles. Seconds later, several heads
were bent together and I got the feeling they were whispering about us.
Not once while at the synagogue did someone
speak the common greeting to me,
"The blessing of the Lord be upon you, we bless you
in the name of the Lord,"
even though we were gone for so long.

But I must look on the brighter side, yes? At least I have
not been commanded to stay in the outer court.

However, as I clutched Yeshua's hand, I yearned to speak
up to all those people who stared so coldly. I wanted to tell
them that there was nothing, absolutely nothing, wrong
with the way dear sweet Yeshua came into the world. His was a pure
and holy conception, but I'm not an abrupt type of
person. Besides, how do you fight a silent enemy?

I sat down beside Shoshoni, who was a
former playmate of mine,
but she turned her shoulder away from me.
Shoshoni's mother is a cousin to my father-in-law.
Would they have
gossiped about me? After a while, Yeshua
crawled into my lap and snuggled
in my arms. I rested my chin against His soft dark
curls and prayed for the ability to forgive.

A rabbi arose and was handed one of the scrolls,
bringing my thoughts back to the present.
A reverential hush
fell over the synagogue,
but I was having trouble concentrating.

*Oh Lord El Elohim Yahweh make Your Son oblivious to the evil
stares, the snide remarks of the cold-hearted, and please,* I added,
from the bottom of my heart, *please, help me to be a good mother.*

Eventually, Yeshua fell asleep,
my arms grew rather weary so I tried to prop him up
beside me. He did not awaken but laid His head against
Shoshoni's arm while His hand rested lightly on her lap.
Oh, that made me cringe. For so long now,

Shoshoni had been making scathing remarks about me thinking
I was so wise because my dohd taught me how to read. Having
Yeshua just gave her more mean things to talk about.
She stiffened and pulled away from our little boy.
My heart nearly broke when He woke up, gave her a
puzzled look, then rested his head on my lap.

****

We barely got into our dark, slightly fusty-smelling
house last night before Shabbat began.
The sun was slipping behind the horizon, the final
blast of the *Shofar*, ram's horn, was fading
when Yosef shook out the pallets and laid them on the sleeping benches.

Imma must have heard that a caravan was coming to town
from Egypt and suspected that we would be with it.
She had a small fire going in the brazier and had everything laid
out in preparation for the lighting of the Shabbat candles. How
it warmed my heart to know she had prepared for our arrival.

Yosef and I had leaned towards each other as I lit the candles,
the first one for him, because he is my husband, the
next for Yeshua, and lastly, one for myself.
We closed our eyes and gently moved our hands over the flames,
while sweeping the warmth towards us.
It was such a blessed experience to be lighting the Shabbat candles
once more in our own homeland
and wafting our prayers up to El Elohim
along with thousands of others of like precious faith.

This is part of what is recited by thousands of lips on the eve of the
Shabbat: *"Blessed art Thou HaShem, King of the Universe, who sanctifies us
with His commandments, and encourages us to light the candles of Shabbat."*

Eventually, we must unpack and get settled in; but for
today, we will relax and enjoy *Yahweh's* holy day.

Oh my, would the Pharisees condemn me if they
knew I take up my reed pen on the Shabbat?

Imma had placed a fresh loaf of challah bread on the table.
It was wrapped in crisp white linen, ready for our Shabbat breakfast.

Sand had also been recently sprinkled on the floor and swept
into pretty swirling designs. That looks like Hanalei's artistry.

What a loving family! At first light, I discovered someone had also
put wild flowers in a pitcher to freshen the house for the Shabbat.

Now I understand why the house had as sweet a
fragrance as it did, in spite of our long absence.

Imma had us over for the repast after the service.
As we sank into the lotus position around the low table once
again, Imma beamed at us all. Now that I am a imma, I am
beginning to grasp how much she loves us. But then, she is so
gracious and welcoming, everyone feels blessed in her presence!

Soon, we will have to break bread with Yosef's parents.
I guess I can bear it.

My little sisters, Dorcas and Naomi, were so happy
to see our little boy. They chattered and giggled
incessantly until Imma hushed them for prayer.

While Imma and I were serving Abba,
Hanalei was shyly holding hands with her young husband using
one hand, while offering him choice morsels of food with the
other. She had married *Caleb bar-Reuven* while we were still in Egypt.

It is our custom to have our men eat first,
Hanalei was constantly hovering over Caleb to make sure
he lacked nothing.

I wonder if Abba had planned to be sternly aloof towards
our little *riba* of so-called questionable birth.
He has not been as accepting as I had hoped he would be by now.
Yeshua had crawled into his lap and stroked his long, flowing black
beard which is now threaded with silver, before the meal, already.

"Are you my *Zaidi*, (Grandfather)?" He asked.

Abba acknowledged that it was so.

"I am glad, "cause you are good *Zaidi*," Yeshua said,
snuggling up under his chin.

I could not be sure, because I was filling a pitcher with
goats milk just then but it looked like Abba
gave Yeshua a little squeeze before He slid off His
Zaidi's lap, and scampered off to play.

When I watch my little sisters, I marvel at how carefree they are.
I was also that way not so very long ago, but the last three
years have been difficult for me and I have changed.

Please, HaShem, may the changes be for the good.
May, I be a caring, compassionate aant'at.

My family was curious about our sojourn in Egypt, as
well as the trip back, and asked many questions.
I am sure if Imma would've know what had happened in Beth
Lechem and our hasty flight to Egypt almost as soon as it happened,
her every thought would have been a plea for our safety.

Later, while we were washing the dishes, we got to
talking about this time, and she turned to Hana.
"Hanalei, don't you recall how we talked often about
Mary'am and Yosef during that time?"
Hana nodded, looked thoughtful.
"I remember you were so burdened.
Every day you would ask Abba to please mention them in prayer."
She paused and absently traced the pattern around
the clay bowl in her hands.

"I remember how often you would stop what you were
doing and stare at nothing in particular. Somehow I knew,
even as a young girl, that you were deep in prayer."

"Aye, do you recall how your cousin, Abigail,
responded when we heard that the babes in
Beth Lechem had been slain?"
Hanalei nodded.
"She was so distraught! In such a un-Abigail-like way,
she burst into the house without calling out first
and flung herself into your arms."

Imma nodded and looked at me.
"She was so sure our, our little Yeshua had been…taken."
I looked down and bit my trembling lip
when I saw Imma's lovely dark eyes glisten with tears.
"She could hardly forgive herself for not being
more kind to you before, before…"
My mother's voice trailed off but we shared
warm, tender looks, knowing each what the other was thinking.

How the memories tumbled around in my head! Especially about
that terrifying escape from Beth Lechem in the shadowy darkness.
A little while later, I noticed Yosef skipping lightly over the part
about the desert storm, and he said nothing at all about
the danger of snakes.

That's good. Why should we frighten our loved ones unduly?
To be sure, I expect to hear him elaborate in greater detail
about some of our scary experiences to the men-folk
when they come to the
carpenter shop.

Our adventures will spin a thrilling tale to the
background sounds of hammer, chisel and saw.

23ʳᵈ Adar

March 6ᵗʰ

DEAR DIARY,

With tears in my eyes, I confided to *Yosef* about how people were still
saying unkind remarks about Yeshua's birth.
I sensed, before our sweet *tinoki* was born, that Yosef was still
somewhat unsure of who the father was, but not anymore.
When I told him about the ridicule, his jaw
hardened and he got a grim look in his eyes.

"This cannot go on," he declared. "From now on,
He will be called Yeshua *bar Yosef*!"
"B-But is He?" I stammered.
"Yes, He will be," he said firmly, "by adoption."
Yosef got some teasing about waiting so long to admit it,
but I know not how he answered the taunting remarks.

25th Adar

March 7th

DEAR DIARY,

I wish I could find more time to write, but here is a little conversation
I will quickly insert while the soup is simmering.

*"Imma, we will go see my little friends in Goshen
again, yes? May we go after night time?"*

Yeshua was standing beside me at the time, while I
carefully added embroidered detail to the bodice
of a new frock I was making for myself. I looked at my fair
young lad who had been leaning his head against my arm.

*"Do you not recall how long it took to come, and
how dry, and dusty the desert was?"*

Yeshua nodded vigorously. "Oh, but I do, Imma, dear. I am bigger
now so sometimes when I ride on the donkey with you, I will hold
your mantle to keep the sun and the sand out of your eyes."

I hid a smile, not knowing if, and how long his
zealous intentions would actually last.

"Abba is much too busy, tinoki. He has to make yokes
and tool handles and other things for people."

Yeshua looked dejected. "But I think Ka-Assai-gen
and—Sic-Na-Mor are lonesome for me. They will be
wondering if I will ever come back. I used to pull baby
Maya-cum Tuu in my cart and I can't no more."
"Anymore," I reminded him gently.

Marilyn Friesen

"Anymore," He repeated humbly as I rested His little
hand on my abdomen. "Remember, son?"
"Is that our baby in there?" He asked. "I think I feel him kick. Why
does he kick you, Imma? Does it hurt? Did I kick you, Imma?"
He threw His arms around my neck. "I did not mean to hurt you.
I do not want to ever, ever hurt you.
I a'Ahava you."

I pressed His sweet tanned cheek into the hollow of my shoulder
while my heart overflowed with warmth for this gentle lad.
He kissed me fervently on both cheeks, copying Yosef, then
said again, "I do not want to ever hurt you, Imma."
I squeezed him a little tighter and looked into His clear,
thoughtful eyes.

"My son, I am sure you do not want to," I whispered.
My heart squeezed, because when He suffers, I suffer also,
somehow I knew that these days of almost idyllic bliss would
end like the clashing of cymbals in a time of deepest sorrow.

What would precede this time of severe suffering,
I knew not, nor how I would survive the darkness
that I cannot foresee, so I wistfully cuddled my darling
for a moment, wishing I could prolong the
day He must leave the security and protection of our happy home.

He stroked my cheek gently and then asked if He could go.
I consented and watched Him scamper off to play
with Thomas, one of his little companions.
I knew they were hoping to get Yosef to help them build a cart
for Dito, the billy goat to haul things . . . if Dito was willing!

I gazed after Him long after He was removed from
my line of vision.
I could hear His sweet high treble calling to His father.

I had thought, *"Yea, you may go, son, but oh Lord El Elohim, Yahweh, it will be so hard to truly let Him go when He is older and must face the wine-press alone.* Oh my, where did that thought come from, what does it ever mean?

I must go. Yosef told me yesterday that I spend too much time pondering things, then I do not get my work done as quickly as I ought. I do want to be a virtuous woman. I must be, Yeshua will need to have the very best upbringing that is humanly possible. *Oh HaShem, have mercy on your unworthy servant, come to her aid.*

9th Tammuz
June 17th

Dear Diary,
Life has gotten so busy now that I have more precious darling babies to care for. I forgot all about this scroll until I dug deep into my trunk in search of baby clothes and there it was!

I really should be weeding in the garden but I will quickly record what happened this morning.

"I have piped unto you, and you have not harkened," A high, girlish voice pouted just outside my window. It was hot even for the month of *Tammuz*, I wondered if that was what was making one of Yeshua's little friends sound so irritable.

With a pottery dish that I had been drying in one hand, I leaned forward to see what was going on. As usual, several of the local children were congregated together with Yeshua, playing in the sand pile. Eight-year-old Rizpah was addressing Asher, Reuven, Yochanam and our *tinoki* with her little hands firmly planted on her small hips.

I watched as Yeshua poured water into the sand, then scraped it flat with a board from the carpenter shop. He had carefully

traced several letters starting with *alef,* the others were copying
them with small twigs clutched in their olive-brown hands.

"I am teaching my friends Hebrew *alef bet,"* (alphabet) He
explained kindly. "We care not to play funeral right now."
Rizpah stamped her foot, out came her lower lip.
"But we need a *rebbe*! Jesse is all dead now, he is on the bier
already but there is no *rebbe* to call out the good he has done.
Yeshua, you make the best *rebbe*. We need you."
Yeshua sighed and looked at His friends.
"Shall we go help with the funeral?"
Yeshua's cousin, Yochanam, jumped up and
brushed the sand off His clothes.
He was a fisherman's son, visiting for the day and
didn't care much for letters and numbers.
Sure," he cried, "I will help carry the bier.
Reuven, you may carry the other end."

"No! Haddam is!" Rizpah flared hotly, giving Yochanam a push.
"Jeremy and Haddam are pall-bearers." Then her face brightened, "But
you can be a zaidi, (grandfather) an' use a cane an' groan loudly!"

They trouped down the street with Rizpah
marching ahead of all the rest. My heart swelled with
love as I watched the little possession trot by.

16th Elul

September 3rd

DEAR DIARY,

Yosef came in for a drink of water during the time of day I usually rest.
He was deeply concerned when he saw me on my knees
addressing the HaShem as my Heavenly Father out loud! I
had gotten into the habit quite unconsciously because Yeshua
loves to call the Creator, Father, which of course He is.

Yosef, with deep concern, admonished me to be very,
very careful about how I address *HaShem*.
He warned me that *El'Elyon* is so High and Holy,
that He is so far above us that we dare not address
Him in a casual or disrespectful way.
Some people have been stoned to death for speaking
of *HaShem* in a light or irreverent manner.

This is something that Yosef must feel
very strongly about because he
even got out the scroll in the middle of his busy work day
to show me what the Torah and the prophets have to say about *HaShem*.

Isaiah taught us that:
"His thoughts are not our thoughts, nor His ways our ways. For
as the Heavens are higher than the earth, so are my ways higher
than your ways, and my thoughts than your thoughts."

Does not our father, David, and others address *El Shaddai* as their
Father? I didn't speak my objections out loud. Perhaps only
religious leaders and kings can take such liberties. Oh dear,
I hope I am not doing something unspeakably wrong by
referring to the Holy One so often in my scrolls.

Please, El'Shaddai, *don't consider me disrespectful! I love you so much!*

Yosef kissed me tenderly when he saw the bleak look on my face
and tried to reassure me that I would be forgiven.
Apparently, Mosheh taught that if a wife or daughter vows a vow,
and it is annulled by her husband or father,
Adonai will not hold her to it.
Yosef felt that this would surely fall into the same category.

. . . And yet my hand is trembling as it moves across the page.
It feels like a heavy, thick curtain
has fallen between me and the Fa…, I mean Yahweh.
Perhaps that is how it is meant to be although I yearn for
the pure innocent communion I knew as a child.
I guess the veil in the temple is symbolic of
our relationship with El Elohim.

Thankfully, in my innocence,
HaShem has allowed me to be comforted by His Shekinah,
for a brief moment, but now that I know better,
I will show Him the deepest respect and refrain from calling him my
Father. Oh, I do hope that it is alright to write about *HaShem*, the
name. My heart aches with a longing for a closer walk with Him!

Is this how Chava felt after she was cast out of the garden?
I suppose she must have felt unbearable sorrow when she
thought of the separation she had caused between mankind
and its wonderful Creator.
She must have also felt so lonely, so bereft when she remembered
how *Elohim* once walked and talked with them in the cool of the day.

I wonder how *HaShem*, hallowed be His Name, wants His
only Son to address Him. When Yeshua is all grown up,
will He make it possible for us weak
sinful mortals to have a meaningful relationship with the Father—I
mean *Yahweh?*

What is the cause for this dark heavy cloud weighing down
on my spirit when I think of Yeshua bridging the gap?
It is so oppressive that I can't bear to be alone one minute longer.

Since I last wrote in my diary, I had gone outside to attach a few vine
tendrils that were straying away from the yarn ladder I had put up
against the house. I'd also gathered our few eggs. There is a dark,
threatening cloud on the horizon. I wish that Yosef would hurry
home. He had to make a delivery across town for a crippled elder.

Maybe the brewing storm was the only reason for my
apprehension. I hope so. After all, *Mashiach* is supposed
to reign as a powerful King . . . is He not?

19ᵗʰ Elul

September 6ᵗʰ

DEAR DIARY,

On the wall in front of me, I have placed a parchment held in place with four sturdy thorns from the Rose of Sharon. A rose bud pierced through with the thorns is drying in each corner. It is a beautiful thought, even though I dare not address El Elohim as my Heavenly Father, it is still a comfort to me.

Perhaps, if I show loving-kindness to all I meet, He will bless me, yes?

The Lord bless thee and keep thee. The Lord make His face shine upon thee and be gracious unto thee. The Lord lift up His countenance upon thee and give thee peace.

PRE–YOM KIPPER

*Y*om *Kippur* is drawing nigh, I can tell by the scriptures *Yosef* chooses
that it is weighing heavily on his heart.

Tonight he read from the Holy Scroll about how the children
of Yisrael prepared themselves for Yahweh's appearance on
Mount Sinai. Yeshua sat at *Yosef's* feet with His arms wrapped
around His legs and listened with wonder and attentiveness.

Yaakov wriggled on my lap, not at all concerned about what happened
so long ago. The story struck such fear into my heart that I
was hardly even aware of *Yaakov's* restlessness. It
lingered with me long after I went to bed.

Then I dreamed we were part of the multitude
at the foot of the mountain.
A thick dark cloud of smoke, shot through with arrows of
lightning, hung over Mount Sinai, the earth shuddered with
the sound of thunder. Everything was a queer dusky green.

In my dream, *Yaakov* struggled to get out of my arms, then abruptly
broke from my grasp. Yeshua saw my alarm and tackled him just
as he reached the roped-off section. He held the howling boy down
until *Yosef* could rescue him. The rope was swaying fearfully.

Seconds later, Asher's *kelev* raced across the boundary barking loudly;
before our horrified eyes, he flopped forwards and was dead!

Aside from the abruptly halted movements of the *kelev*, there
was an oppressive stillness permeating the air. It was so chilling
that I woke up with beads of cold sweat on my brow.

How, I worried, can we ever satisfy a El Elohim so mighty
and holy that He could strike us down with a look?

How is it that our Yeshua feels so . . . comfortable in His
Shekinah? Is it just because He is a child, His child? *Mosheh*,
was one of the greatest leaders our people has ever known,
was not even allowed to see *HaShem's* face, lest he die!

During the following few evenings, *Yosef* solemnly quoted the Ten
Commandments, two each night, carefully explaining each one so that
at least Yeshua could understand.
You should have seen how wide-eyed
our small son was. I found myself trembling. How can I be sure I have
not fallen short of complete obedience?
I know I have in my thoughts countless times.
How sternly will *HaShem* judge us for our meditations?

When we lighted the candles that Friday eventide,
I think our prayers were more solemn, more earnest than
usual. We fell to our knees while Yosef lead in prayer.

When we were done, Yeshua turned to me and clasped
my cheeks between the palms of His little hands.

"Imma, it's just like you and Abba," He explained, "you make rules for
us to obey and my Heavenly Father does, too. But because He is EL
Elohim, He gives us the *want* to obey the rules." Surely He is right!

I saw a gentle look in Yosef's eyes as He swung Yeshua up
on his shoulders and hiked off to bed with Him.
I know he enjoys and appreciates
his eldest son very much, even if he feels somewhat
flummoxed at times about how to guide Him.
I gazed upon them with loving pride,
but also with longing in my heart. *Will we someday
be able to have just as warm a relationship with
the Heavenly Father as Yeshua has with both His heavenly
and earthly fathers?* What a strange thought!
Surely, no one but the Mother of the
lovely Christ Child would ever even consider such a possibility.

Cheshvan 19th

November 4th

DEAR DIARY,

Oh what a time of perplexity and anxiety we are now in.
I will put it in Yeshua's own words.
"Imma, why are we going to dohd Gideon's *right
now* and why can't Abba come with us?"
How can I answer the little boy without frightening him unduly?

A caravan arrived in Sepphoris several days ago
, everyone is frantic because diphtheria has swept
among them and it has spread to the city.
Already several people have died! Since the city of Sepphoris is
so near Navara, what happens there naturally affects us.

My mother is among the volunteers bringing food and
comfort to those who are ailing, the poor suffering souls.
So many refuse to help lest they be stricken, also.
Imma, Abba and Yosef, in particular, are urging me to
flee with our little ones, lest we become ill also.

I am just feeling so overwhelmed.
Lydia is only three months old, I am in no condition
to travel so far alone. Yeshua has only reached his fifth year and
His small brother is a rambunctious two years old. I am feeling
careworn about taking this journey without Yosef by my side!

Gideon will soon be at the door with his cart
and donkey so I must go.
His wife, my cousin Salome, and I have been good friends
for many years so it is natural that I would
turn to her in my time of distress.

DEAR DIARY,

Twenty-seven furlongs (nearly four miles) is a long uncomfortable
trip when one is jostling along in the back of a wagon, but at least it is
leading us further away from Sepphoris.
Lydia was fretful and would not settle,
I suppose because she was feeling my tension. Because
she was hungry, she could not sleep either.
Yaakov is at that inquisitive age where he wants to
explore everything. He would have tumbled off countless
times if I had not leaped up, babe in arm, to rescue him.

What made matters ever so much worse was that one time
when I reached out to grab him, somehow my veil got caught
in the spokes of the wheel and the cart lurched to a stop.

It made Gideon exclaim in surprise,
at first, then in annoyance at the delay. It's understandable, of
course, since it is finally dry enough to sow barley and then he had
to come and fetch us. (Whence could we have fled otherwise?)`

Yosef wasn't able to bring us because he had
an unusually large order of trunks
to be shipped to Damascus by the month of *Tevet*. Our Yosef
has gained himself quite a reputation for being one of the best
carpenters in all the surrounding villages, but it still amazes
me that he got such a large order from so far away.

Yosef had a difficult time procuring enough camphorwood for
so many chests. I hoped the cost of purchasing it and having it
delivered wouldn't outweigh what he gets for selling them
but he just smiled and said, "You need not
worry about such things, my love."
Soon, soon, our eager little Yeshua will be
more than just a fetch and carry boy. He wants
so much to do what Abba does.

Generally, He is very attentive to the needs of the little ones,
but today Yeshua was enthralled with the great out of doors,
He would stand first on one side of the cart,
and then the other, trying to take it all in.
He kept up a running commentary on everything
He observed but I was too distracted by Yaakov's antics
to pay much attention.

I'm glad we arrived safely.

DEAR DIARY,

Get on your low stool if needs be, peer through this high,
narrow window so we can watch the children.

"Uncle Gideon, Uncle Gideon,"
Yeshua cried, tugging at Gideon's Hand, "are you ready to go
seeding? May I come? Please, please may I come too?"

Gideon continued to scoop handfuls of seed into the
shoulder bag beside him as looked up with a smile.
"If Rachael is half as enthused as you are about seeding,
I could not imagine not taking you both!"

"*Alvey*! (Would it be so!) Rachael! Rachael! Where are you?" He raced
out of hearing distance, but soon came back dragging Rachael with
him, or maybe it was the other way around, I could not be certain.
Gideon handed them a child's version of his seed bag,
they had a slight tussle over who should carry it.
Gideon suggested that they take turns,
Yeshua readily agreed. Rachael triumphantly
hoisted the bag around her neck. Her
father slowly poured it half-full of grain.
"This is very heavy, "she boasted, "but I am strong!"
"Maybe I should carry it when it's so heavy," Yeshua
suggested, "and you may carry it when it's lighter."
"Nay! *Abba*! Yeshua can carry it first. No! I want to."
"I think you ought to let Him because it is heavy,
and He is your guest."
Rachael looked so very downcast that
Yeshua relented and said, "You may carry it for a little while,
cousin, but when you get too tired, I will help you."

Their voices were fading off into the distance by then
so I hurried out to hear the last of their prattle.

While I was in the yard, I spotted my cousin's
parched-looking bean plants,
they had sprouted only a few days earlier,
so I watered them. I am afraid they had been neglected
because she was so busy with all of us being there.

My eyes strayed often to the threesome fading in
the distance as they walked across the field,
one child merrily swinging on each of Gideon's hands. I was
glad he was so good-natured about them being with him.
I was on my knees, pouring water from a pitcher,,
when quite unexpectedly someone tackled me from behind. A little
yeled, whom I love so much, wrapped his arms around my neck.
"Shalom, Yaakov," I smiled,
"do you want to help me fill the watering pot once
more so we can water Auntie Salome's gourds?"

He nodded enthusiastically and tugged at my
hand to lead me over to the well.
I cast a lingering glance at the children,
they were copying Gideon's wide-sweeping arm swings
to make the seed to spread far and wide.

The freshly plowed ground looks rich and fertile now, but
experience told me there would be thorns, thistles and other
problems which Gideon would find hard to keep up with.

I could not know it at the time, but Yeshua was nattering on
about the rocks in one corner of the field and worrying about the
birds that were flocking behind them to peck at the seeds.

I saw Gideon remove his mantle, causing them to flutter
away. They flew off but soon settled back down
a few cubits off to renew their snacking. Maybe they were thinning it
out where the seed had fallen too thickly, yes? We can only hope so.

We knew the *farmers* would be hot, hungry and thirsty by the
time the sun was high in the sky, so Salome and I prepared a lunch
and drew fresh cold water from the well in the heat of the day.

With a vessel of water crowning my head, Lydia asleep on my
back, and a basket of victuals as Salome's crown, we sashayed
across the field with our toddlers scampering at our sides. I love to
watch our little children. They are still so innocent, so carefree.

We had a picnic near some oleander bushes beneath an
oak tree while fluffy clouds drifted lazily in the sky.
The air was fragrant with the heady smell of freshly turned soil.
If Yosef could have been here, it
would have been perfect. Yosef is so much heart of my heart,
he is never far from my thoughts.

We took Yeshua and Rachael home with us for naps
after lunch, and they both fell asleep promptly.
Nay, I did not say that quite right.
They both protested vigorously, but after being covered
with light blankets, they quickly fell asleep.

I am sure Yeshua will be more than ready to go along with his
uncle tomorrow morning . . . and the next, and the next.

I'd say that He would make a wonderful farmer but on the other hand
he is just as enthused about helping Yosef in the carpenter shop.

He loves to make crude little toys to play with in the sandbox.
I'd never tell Him that I called them that, but I am not always sure
what they are. His friends are always delighted with them.
Asher also, likes to make things from scraps of leftover wood,
so the two of them have great fun building together.

*Thank you, oh thank you, Adonai, for giving
our children a happy childhood.*

DEAR DIARY,

While on the way home, we were hurrying down this
barren empty road because it was showering, suddenly, the worst,
most cruel scene known to man loomed over the next hill.

Before I knew what He was up to, Yeshua scrambled over the edge
of the cart, racing over to this man who was writhing on a cross!

Even I, having never seen such an appalling sight before,
stiffened with horror; my young, innocent son was
already encountering humanity at its worst!

Because Gideon had stopped to dislodge a stone in the frog of
the donkey's hoof, Yeshua had managed to leap off so quickly.

We both called out to Him, but there was a clap of thunder right
then, his little brown legs kept scurrying down the road.

Gideon leaped up onto the cart bench and urged
the donkey closer to the pitiful scene.

Yeshua, our little Yeshua, stood beside a gnarled old tree on which
was pinioned a suffering man, His hands were clasped entreatingly.

In spite of stumbling on the hem of my dress, in spite of
Lydia clutching my shawl in her chubby little fist and nearly
blinding me, I managed to get to Him surprisingly quickly.

When I saw how torn the criminal's wrists were, where the
nails had been driven in, my stomach heaved and before
I knew it I was vomiting right there on the road.

Marilyn Friesen

When I looked up to wipe my face on the scrap of
material tucked in my cloth belt, there were tears
coursing down Yeshua's smooth innocent cheeks.

"Oh, please, Soldiers," He entreated, "could you not
take him down, now? He has such terrible *owies*."

The two youthful soldiers glanced nervously at
each other, shuffled their feet uneasily.

"Please, Sir, I know not what he did. I suppose it was
very naughty, but I think he is sorry now."

He looked up at the captive who had been about to gasp out
some snide remark. "You are, are you not?" Yeshua asked. The
criminal belatedly jerked his head in an up and down motion.
"See, he's *nephal*."
"Look, brat, we are just obeying orders. This is no place for
you anyway, so beat it," one of the guards retorted angrily.

"But, but, he will . . . he will die!" Yeshua sobbed.
I reached out imploringly to my little child,
"Yeshua, my son," I cried, "this is no place for my little *tinoki*.
Come with Imma!"
He obediently took my hand, His eyes were
deep pools of sadness.

As much as I wished He would not do so,
Yeshua stood at the back of the cart and gazed at the
sad scene until it was only a smudge on the
horizon.
Why must it trouble Him so?

Sometimes, I almost wish He did not have quite such
a tender heart because it causes Him such pain.

When He finally did sit down, it was with His tanned arms
wrapped around His knees, as He gazed at nothing in particular.
I wished He would share what was on His heart,
maybe I could help Him.
But perhaps the pain was too deep to put into words.
He just sat there with His head on His knees with
a faraway look in His eyes, I wept for Him.

DEAR DIARY,

Yeshua was sadly subdued all last week. Oh, I pray He can forget
this tragic incident, to enjoy life like a little boy should.
If only they would not crucify criminals along roadsides!
But I suppose they do it as a warning to others. It is not
only Yeshua who has been quiet and sad. I am also.
Yosef was dismayed when he heard what we
had encountered. I suspect he has seen it often in his travels, but has
chosen not to tell me. Oh, if only I could get on to other subjects.

DEAR DIARY,

No one said being a mother would be easy, but it is sure worth it.

Take a peek inside our little abode this evening.
Both boys had had their feet washed and were tucked into
bed. Lydia had finally fallen asleep in her father's arms;
Yosef smiled tenderly while looking at his peacefully sleeping daughter.
I was sipping a glass of buttermilk beside him
when one of the little boys called. Yosef and I exchanged
weary glances.

"I went last time," Yosef reminded me with a gentle smile.

"Yea, I know." Yaakov had called thrice already asking for a cup of
water and hugs, but we knew he was just prolonging the inevitable.

Now, Yeshua's youthful voice floated through the dusky stillness.

I slipped through the curtained-off partition
and settled myself on the edge of their bed. After tucking the
blanket, that my mother and I had so lovingly woven, around
his shoulders, I took His hand and stroked it gently.
"What is it, son?" I asked, brushing His long
thick tendrils off His forehead.
"Is Yaakov Yahweh's son also?" His incredibly
green eyes looked searchingly into mine.
My heart skipped a beat. *El Shaddai*,
I wasn't expecting this! How do I answer him?

"Yaakov is my son, just like you are, but Yosef is his Abba."
Yeshua's brows knit together. "Why can't I see My Father?"

Marilyn Friesen

"Because He lives in Paradise; because He is *Adonai,* He
can see you, my son, even if You can't see Him."

I closed my eyes for a moment, trying to imagine what part of
the Creation Yeshua would most identify with. "He reminds
us of His *Shekinah* in every stalk of corn that cradles
a jewel of dew, and in every frolicking lamb.
He is the One that made beautiful rainbows and
snow-white clouds."

I could see that He wasn't quite satisfied, "He sent
Abba to care for you." I reminded Him gently.

"But I love my Father!" He flung His arms out in an impetuous
gesture, nearly hitting me in the nose without even noticing. "I
love talking to Him, Imma. I want to see Him. He's my Abba!"

Oh, dear, I had reconciled myself with the thought of
not addressing *HaShem,* (hallowed be His Name), too
familiarly and now the topic was coming up again!

I marvel at His clear bright-eyed confidence in His Father's care.

I heard Yosef's muffled footfalls on the hard packed dirt
floor behind me, I looked up as he held back the curtain to
peer around it. Lydia was still sleeping on his shoulder.

"What's the matter?"

"Yeshua was just telling me how much he loves
talking to His Heavenly Father."

Yosef shook his head seriously. "Oh no, my son,
you mustn't address Him as your Abba."

Yeshua had shifted into a kneeling position on the bed,
now He lifted His clasped hands entreatingly.

"But He is my Father!"

"But He is also . . ." Yosef's voice dropped to a
hushed whisper, "The Holy One! *HaShem*!"

"Can't I talk to Him?"

"Yea, but . . ." Yosef glanced at Yaakov,
he seemed to be wondering how it would affect his other
son if Yeshua freely referred to HaShem as His father.

"I like talking to Him. He loves me!"
Yosef and I cast each other troubled glances. After all, He is *Yahweh's*
son. "You must always talk to Him very, very respectfully. Do you
know what it means to pray respectfully?"

Yeshua nodded vigorously. "Oh, I will, I will. I love Him and I
want to always be kind to Him. I want to pray right now!"
"Shh!" we chorused. "Yaakov and Lydia are sleeping," I reminded Him.
"Then I will pray quietly right here,"
He declared. He squeezed His eyes shut and knelt
right there on the middle of His pallet.

As we backed out of the room, we listened as Yeshua's
clear sweet voice addressed *HaShem*.

*"Dear Heavenly Father. I a'Ahava you very, very much.
I want to always be a good boy and please you. I am glad you are
my Abba. You make such nice things for us to look at. Amen."*

Yosef and I looked at each other wonderingly.
Surely, *HaShem* would
accept such child-like worship even it didn't follow all the rules laid
down for us. I took Lydia from her Abba's arms and tucked her into
the cradle bed. I stroked her downy head with my finger.

Mothering two small sons is wonderful, but there is something
uniquely special about having my own little daughter to care for.
While giving the cradle a push with my foot, I was reminded
of another baby, tinier than she is now, who had only
a manger for His first bed.
What a magnificent but difficult time those days had been.
I knew I would always be in awe concerning
the days surrounding Yeshua's birth.

DEAR DIARY,

Hmmm, It's pretty quiet around here. I wonder what the boys are up
to. I finished making the soup for dinner, checked to see if baby Lydia
was still asleep, then wandered outside. James (Yaakov) was close by. He
called to me, I duly admired what he was building in the sand pile with
scraps of lumber from the carpenter's shop.
"Where's Yeshua,"
"He went to yonder woods to feed the little folk," his brother solemnly
replied as he stuck a row of sticks in the ground. What a perfect day
to be out of doors. I walked eagerly down the path to *yonder* woods.
Since no one was around, I took the liberty to remove my
shawl and drape it over my arm. The breeze felt good as it
lifted and played with my long, dark cascading locks.
Soon, I heard the lilting, childlike voice of my small son.
Stepping softly, lest I would accidentally snap a twig and
send his little friends scurrying away, I crept closer.
"Don't be so greedy, bar crow. I want wee sparrow to get some,
also. You are scaring her away. Oh, *Shalom*, little starling.
Would you like some to?
One, two, three, four, five, which ones are missing?
Oh, *Shalom, bar tamarin.* I see you brought your wife
along today."
He grinned widely as the little monkey scampered up a
tree just above His head and swung on a branch
until the leaves brushed against Yeshua's hair. I watched
as my son stretched His arm out and scratched on the
dirt to invite a shy mole to come in closer.

I beamed with joy as all the fluttering, scurrying creatures
crowded around Him and hadn't guessed that there were so
many just a stone's throw from the edge of our land.

He picked them up each one and caressed them, I got a
lump in my throat seeing how much they trusted.
Pretty soon, I saw the yellow eyes of a fox gleaming
in the greenery. *Oh-oh, here comes trouble.*
Oh, Shalom, mama fox. You are welcome to join us if you
behave yourself. You will behave yourself, won't you?"
I was amazed to see the fox look down as if ashamed,
or maybe embarrassed, then sidle in closer, but I was
not surprized that the little ones all scattered
until Yeshua gently coaxed them to return.
As Yeshua handed out bread crumbs, I understood why we had
been so short of bread lately. Oh, well it would be no problem
to bake a extra for his little companions from now on.
Yeshua, " I called softly, "it is getting late, we need
to eat. You will come with me now, yes?"
My son instantly got up and brushed the crumbs from his
garments. He slipped His little hand in mine and chattered
happily as we returned to the house. But I, as His mother,
kept all these things and pondered them in my heart.

DEAR DIARY,

I don't know if I should be embarrassed to insert this.
My cousin, Abigail, stopped in to
borrow a couple eggs just when I was getting Yeshua ready for
school and she later handed this to me. (It is in her Abba's script.)
I'm sure she just wanted to *be* there for and with me at this momentous
time, especially since she hasn't been blessed with children of her own.
Our friendship has blossomed once again, for which I thank *El Adonai*.

ABIGAIL'S ADDITIONS

There was a tender look in Mary'am's eyes as she watched her small son slip his hand into Yosef's large, calloused one. He skipped along as carefree as a lark down the dusty, village street while the muted light of early dawn cast a glow on the white mud-brick houses and nearby palm trees.

As sure as her given name was Mary'am, she knew that no longer would Yeshua be her baby, but he would grow up and away from her. Today, at five, he was skipping off to the synagogue school for the first time, so totally unafraid. It was she that had the mixed emotions. It was she that longed to hold him close just a little bit longer, but nay, he must go, and grow, and there was nothing she could do about it but hope for the best and pray for his safety.

Safety; Mary'am shuddered and drew her shawl
closer although it was not a cold day.

How well she remembered the terrifying night when they fled to Egypt. He was just a wee lad, then. Not even out of his swaddling clothes, and they had to pack with such haste and escape with their lives while the shouts of soldiers, screams of mothers, and wails of babies ricocheted all around them. Then Mary'am's panicky breathing slowed. *HaShem* had protected them then, and He would protect them now. After all Yeshua was His Son; His only begotten son.

A small hand was tugging at her garments, and a plaintive voice penetrated her consciousness. James was up and getting hungry. As she tended to the needs of the little ones, prepared the daily bread and tended the chickens and goat, her thoughts wended off down to that orderly synagogue school.

It was so easy to picture Yeshua sitting there, cross-legged
like all the rest, in a semi-circle around their teacher.

She frowned slightly. *I do hope that the school master will
be patient with him if he speaks out of turn. He is such a
bright, inquisitive lad that it will be hard to restrain himself
when a question pops into his dark, curly head.*

Yosef stooped to enter the door right then, and he reached for the
Torah as Mary'am laid out the breakfast food on the table. It was
rare for them to eat without their eldest son, but since this was
his very first day at the synagogue school they thought it best if
he ate a little earlier so that he would get there in plenty of time.
During a lull in the childish prattle that filled their two
room house, Mary'am thought she could hear the
chanting of a dozen voices floating down the street.
She smiled gently. " Yeshua is in good hands, and when
he comes home his father and I will continue to nurture
and guide him to the very best of our ability."

27th Av

August 27th

DEAR DIARY,

I gently rerolled the scroll and placed it out of reach of inquisitive little fingers so that I could show it to Yosef later.

"Abigail," I said, "thank you. You are so sensitive to my emotions. Thank you for writing this out for me. Thank you for sharing it. It will be a treasured memory.

DEAR DIARY,

I repositioned *Yaakov'* head against my shoulder and wondered how long he had been sleeping. The story had been more for Yeshua anyway. He seemed so wise, so discerning for His age.

"Why wouldn't the *aant'at* believe?"

"Maybe they did, in their own way, but they weren't brought up as carefully as Noah's sons."
will record for you now the memories of one of our most interesting evenings.

"Imma, dear," Yeshua pleaded, carefully wrapping His arms around me because I was great with child, "tell us the story of the flood," He begged, "and tell it like you were really there. I like that the best."

"Wait awhile until I finish getting Jose to sleep," I replied softly as I rocked him gently in my arms. His flingers fluttered outside of the blanket at the sound of my voice, then he relaxed again.

Soon I laid him down and his big brothers snuggled up on either side of me.

"Remember, this is a pretend story. I was not really there, so no not know how it truly happened, but this is how I imagine it to have been.

"Noah sadly turned around and walked to the yawning door of the ark. Then he looked back and beckoned one more time.

"'Come,'" he pleaded, with outstretched hands, "'will not you come into the ark, and be saved? It is nearly done, and truly a great flood will come and wash you all away.'

"As usual, they laughed derisively, and, as was happening more and more lately, some threw stones so Noah had to duck inside to be safe.

"A short distance away, able-bodied men were clambering all over the framework of a tall building that was rapidly going up. They hadn't even bothered to come and listen.

"Noah was aware that a huge party was expected to take place later in the evening, it was to last for several days.

"With deep sorrow, Noah shook his hoary head and thought, *Oh, Lord, how can I convince them? What more can I say? I have used every type of entreaty I can think of. So many think they are far too urbane to listen to an ignorant country preacher like myself.*

"'It has never rained, it never will,'" they keep shouting at him.

"Noah had been building on the ark for well over one hundred years. Perhaps it was taking so long because more and more of the workmen were quitting. The scorn of their comrades was more than they wanted to bear.

"'I'll soon be quitting, although it's not that I mind working for him,'" one young man confided to his brother. "'He treats us kindly, and gives us a reasonable wage, but I'm just so sick and tired of *Sakra-lotin* and his gang beating up on me for being Noah's hired man.'"

"*Jare-daeki* nodded in agreement. "'I admire the old crony, but I wouldn't be caught dead inside that boat after it's all finished. It's really insane what Noah is doing, although he seems so sincere, poor guy.'

"'Here, take the other end of this plank.'"

I paused then gently stroked Yeshua's cheek. "Or maybe he was deliberately taking his time to give as many as possible the opportunity to find shelter when the Great Flood did come."

Yeshua nodded thoughtfully, snuggled in closer.

I wondered if the sophisticated ones were
embarrassed when they saw that
big hulk of an ark. Did they just go to and fro as usual from their
businesses and places of entertainment with only an occasional look at
the ark, or could it be that they complained to their leaders that such
an eyesore should be removed. It was a disgrace to their fine city.

It was getting cool in the house so I tucked
a blanket around the three of us.

"Don't you think Noah was getting lonely because so many of
his relatives and friends, who had also worshipped the true El
Elohim, had already passed away?" I continued after settling
down, flanked by two of my wonderful sons. "Some
had died natural deaths, but all too many had suffered at the hands of
violent men."

"Noah's three robust sons were a big help, but each of them had
found a wife recently and that that slowed them down."
"Why, Imma?"
"Why, what?"
"...would having a wife slow them down?"
"Oh, they would rather sit around and visit with their wives than
build on the ark. At least that's what I think."
Yeshua wrinkled His nose. "Not me, I'd rather build on something
any day! I like being a carpenter, besides *talithas* are so boring.
Except not you, Imma dear," he added hurriedly,
"but then you're not *a talitha;* you are an *aant'at.*"

"Sometimes, Noah wondered how much those young wives believed in what he was doing," I continued, "especially the one . . ."

Yeshua snuggled closer, "Tell me more, Imma."

"I'll pretend to be one of the wives now.

"I was standing a short distance behind Father Noah as he spoke to the people, I could see conviction working on some of the faces, but no one responded.

"One young talitha wanted to come into the ark but her father forcibly restrained her. She looked worried.

"Noah waited a long time but no one stepped forward.

"With a sob in my throat, I turned when he turned, and we went to help tie the animals into their stanchions. They had been filing in all day in pairs or in groups of seven, and the others had been kept busy keeping order.

"At first, the multitude had cheered and joked about the animals traipsing by as if they thought it was some amusing spectacle, but eventually the laughter died down.

"I don't think they wanted to watch any more. Did it make them feel uncomfortable? Did some wonder if the animals were wiser than they?

"One agile youngster shimmied up into a coconut palm and shouted; "If your puny rain does come, I'll be safe." It caused several others to try to climb, also but it is not as easy as it looks. Besides, he flung green coconuts down at them.

"After a while, a powerful sound of creaking and groaning prevailed over all other sounds. It almost caused my heart to stop beating when I stared at that massive door rolling shut without the aid of human hands, but I was so glad to be on the inside!

"When the door was half way down, I glimpsed the terrified, white faces of two young talitha. I called out to them, but they clasped hands and ran way. It was too late for me to run after them. Because they wanted to, and were young, surely El'Elyon will pardon them."

Yeshua nodded solemnly, but I hardly noticed
as I continued my narrative.
"I turned sadly away and went to help Noah, and the others.
"If I hadn't been so burdened because of the stubbornness
of the people who were going to be lost, I would have
marveled at how orderly most of the animals were.
"Sure, a frisky lamb scampered right past a magnificent
pair of lions almost as if he was taunting them,
but they did not even roar, let alone give chase.
They sedately strolled down the center aisle to their correct stall and
patiently waited while Seth fastened halters around their necks.

"Next to them were the zebras, which I would not have
thought was such a wise plan; beside them were the tigers.
But other than the fact they seemed to have low conversations
going amongst themselves, they were all behaving
amazingly well. But I was too broken-hearted—"

"What does broken-hearted mean, Imma?" Yeshua
whispered with His arms wrapped around my neck.
He'd startled me. I had forgotten His presence.
"Sad, very sad," I pressed a kiss against
His upturned cheek, then continued with my narrative.
"Tears had flooded my eyes, making it hard to
see what I was doing.
My sister-in-law, *Shandeel,* was helping me put the sheep, goats
and their babies into a pen. Zillah was shooing all the birds
into a vast aviary beneath the open window in the roof.

"It was a sight to behold, with all the ducks, geese, chickens, pelicans,
ostriches and other fowl waddling around in the straw below;
parrots, eagles, swans and many other birds were perched
up higher or flying around in their small confines.

"It was truly a miracle that there was no
squabbling or, um, hunting going on."
Yosef had been doing some figuring on a wax tablet. Now
he laid it aside and carefully carried Yaakov to bed.

"Haven't you had enough for tonight?" I asked Yeshua.

"Just a little bit more, please, Imma. I find it so interesting."
I looked at Yosef, our eyes met. He nodded slightly, so I continued.
"'Why don't you sit down and rest for a while, Chava?'" Noah's
wife asked sympathetically when she saw me fumbling with
the latch for the pen that enclosed the small woodland creatures.
I think she knew that I had been feeling emotional.
"I nodded without saying a word and stumbled over
to the table. After collapsing on the bench,
I buried my head in my arms and just cried and cried. I was sitting
so close to the door; I could dimly hear what was going on outside.
Some were mocking, as usual, but they seemed
louder and harsher than before.
"I heard someone close by say something like,
"'Now that the troublemakers are locked inside, how will they
will get out? Looks like their El Elohim tricked them, this
Time, but good.'
"That disrespectful comment was followed by raucous laughter.
By the sound of things, it seemed like most were going
about their activities at their usual frenzied pace.

"As I leaned my head against the sturdy wall, and tried to listen,
I couldn't stop groaning deeply while the tears flowed freely.

"Some of those people I knew and loved! Some
had been my childhood friends,
although in later years they had mocked and scorned me."

"I would have cried too," Yeshua whispered.

I looked into Yeshua's deep, comprehending eyes and
marveled that He had not grown tired of my lengthy
story. He is so perceptive for a boy of nine.

"After a while, Seth, my Abba, put his arm around me."

"Your husband, you mean?" Yeshua said with a knowing smirk.

I nodded and grinned.

"Seth told me it was time to eat so I looked up to
see that simple victuals had been laid out.

"None of us cared much for food, we were
too burdened, worrying about our
Aleichem who had resisted the tender voice of El
Elohim, to think much about eating.

"From time to time, we heard brawling going on.
Somehow it seemed even more violent than usual,
even though muffled by the thick solid walls.

"For seven days, we begged El Elohim to cause someone to repent and
call out for mercy. We were so heavy-hearted that we ate only enough
togive us the minimal strength needed to care for the animals.
It was devastating to think of all those people
stubbornly sinking to their
awful fate, sometimes we wondered if we really
had tried hard enough to convince them."
"Yahweh did not want to do it," Yeshua stated with firm conviction.
"Nay, He certainly did not.
As the first crash of thunder resounded,"
I continued, "Father Noah tramped upstairs to close off the skylight.
"We were plunged into total darkness until Seth, Ham and Japheth
managed to light our lamps which were standing in readiness.

"As the rain poured down, and the thunder crashed, the
animals started trumpeting and squealing, each in their
own language. We womenfolk clung to each other.

"I managed to hear Father Noah's voice above the din, he was
praying that *HaShem* would keep us from fear.

"Gradually, the racket died down, but then I heard something
worse, the cries, screams and curses of those on the outside!
That was more heart-wrenching than the panic of the animals.

"It . . . it was almost more than I could bear."

As I wiped my eyes and blew my nose, I berated myself
for getting so caught up in the stories I tell.

Yeshua wrapped His arms around my waist and
buried His head against my bosom.
I thought this might be too much for him so I fell silent.

"I want to be like Noah when I get big. And tell people about El
Elohim," He said, lifting sober eyes to mine. "Is there more to the story?"

"That's about all, *tinoki,* I am almost finished. Here is the last of it."

"We were kept busy feeding the animals. The men
cleaned the manure along the gutters, then shoved it
down long chutes into the holding pen beneath.
"We became friendly with different animals;
Japheth even taught several of the larger more colorful
birds to talk, which was most entertaining.
Most of them flew away after the flood, but he kept one
as a pet for many years.

"One little lamb refused to stay in its pen, it insisted on
following me up and down the aisles whenever I was
feeding the other animals. I grew attached to him.
"It wasn't as busy as you might think, though,
because after a while, many of the
creatures were lulled to sleep by the constant motion of the ship and
the dimness of their surroundings, we only needed to feed them
occasionally.

We were lonesome and hard, very hard to think of our
friends and neighbors rejecting the call of El Elohim, being
eternally punished because of their neglect and rebellion.
We all had relatives that were left behind, we talked
about them in hushed whispers now and then.
I think Zillah, especially, was becoming resentful
that El Elohim had done that to her family.
"The waters lessened, we eventually reached
dry land and were able to disembark.
I was awestruck with a brilliant rainbow
that was arching across the sky.
It was *Yahweh's* way of promising us that He would
never destroy the world with a flood again.
I was so relieved.

"It felt like my heart broke when my little pet lamb had to be slain
as a sacrifice, it was the only perfect male lamb on the ark."

Just then, the baby let out a loud wail as if something had startled
him, so I quickly concluded the story and scurried to Jose's rescue.

It wasn't until later that night, when I was trying to go to sleep,
that I realized Yeshua's head had dropped into His hands when I
mentioned the lamb, He had remained motionless for a long time.

PURIM

2nd Nisan

March 13th

DEAR DIARY,

Purim arrived at sundown yesterday, with it, Gideon's cart
rattled into our yard. We had decided that since we are poor in earthly
goods, we would give the gift of time to each other.
Purim is one of our most joyous holidays because it is a reminder
of how Esther helped us, perhaps someday, we too will be
relieved of oppression, which in our case would be from the Romans.
Oh what a happy day when our families can get together!
We were so busy visiting that we had not gotten
around to calling the children in when
darkness fell. Yosef and Gideon were nearby in the carpenter shop,
which is attached to the house, so I wasn't worried.
It is so interesting to listen to little children at play, or to hear them
prattle about it later. As usual, my imagination is filling in the details.

"It's getting too dark to play Rodents and Foxes any longer!"
Devora, the chunky little girl from down the street, declared.

"Uh, Uh!" Asher stoutly retorted, "If you're too scared to play in the
Dark, you can go home. It's more exciting in the dark anyways!"
"But we can't see!" Rachael, Salome's daughter, timidly protested.
Asher looked at her kindly. "If you're scared to go by yourself, I will
help you find a hiding place."
My, my, nearly the same words but such a different tone he can use!
"Eek! *Shuah* is still the fox then!"
All the children, except Devora scattered, looking for appropriate
hiding places.
"Hurry, Devora, I am going to get my midnight snack soon!" *Shuah*
threatened before covering his eyes.

Devora walked slowly towards the carpenter shop, which was well lighted with candles and lamps placed here and there. *I know what I will do!* her face brightening. *The Abba's are not looking this way anyway, so I will just borrow one of the candles so I can see.* Almost as soon as the thought flashed through her mind, she was already slipping out the back way with the candle in her hand. *Oh dear, they will see the light, and make a beeline for me.".* She slipped behind the carpenter shop, tucking herself into one of the packing crates. The light flickered brightly in her clasped hands.

Here and there, she heard little *rodents'* scurrying in the dark, an occasional squeal and a giggle. *I am sure they can see my light. What will I ever do? Oh I know! There is one of Mary'am's fruit baskets. I will hide my candle under it.* She beamed proudly at the comforting flame flickering through the narrow slats, but then her eyes grew wide as the light dimmed from lack of air and slowly went out.

Devora's heart thudded. *Now I am in utter darkness.* She nervously chewed on her lip. *They will never ever find me back here! Oh dear, Oh dear, why did I ever find such a scary place to hide?* The shrieks of children being caught gradually subsided.

"Where is Devora?" a young girl by the name of Sarah asked.

"Did she not go home?"

"I think so."

"Let's start another game. Yochanam, you're the fox because I caught you first."

"Children, it's time to come in now!"

I heard a collective groan but if *Devora* wailed loudly,
as the last child's voice faded, no one heard her.

Several minutes later, there was a loud pounding on the door.
"Where's Devora?" A large disheveled matron demanded.
Our own children looked at one another in surprise.
"I thought she had gone home!" Yeshua exclaimed.
"Well, she didn't!" The woman's black eyes flashed.
"She must be still hiding. Come Yaakov, come Jose, let's
go look for her. Do you want to come to, Shimon?"

Uncle Gideon and Yosef joined in the search, each with a lantern, in
short order, the tear-stained talitha was being hauled back home.
A day or two later, Yosef asked the boys to tidy up behind the
carpenter shop, they were quite surprised to find a candle under a
smoke stained bushel basket.

DEAR DIARY,

"**I**mma," Yeshua called as He saw me gathering the sun-dried laundry which was spread out on the grass and anchored down with rocks, "would you have time to tell me a story?"

"*Yaakov*, Lydia and Jose are playing in the woods" the eleven-year-old continued, "Shimon is building something in the sand pile and Ruthie is playing with the doll I made for her. Could you please?"

I smiled fondly at my tall son, He now reached higher than my shoulder. " I will always have time for you, my son. Even if my hands are busy, in my heart I am still listening, thinking and caring for each one of my *tinoki.*"

He sat down in the grass, leaned up against me.
I placed the reed clothes basket nearby.
We could hear the gentle breeze singing a lullaby in the trees. At our feet a million daisies, poppies, tall glorious Lily of the Valley, daffodil and other flowers were dancing in the gusting air currents.

Soon, the hot dry desert winds will come bearing down, this sea of colorful flowers will just be a lovely memory to cherish until another season. So far, they were still lingering. It is a perfect day.

"Which story do you want to hear today?" I asked, and was surprised that His face sobered instantly.

"I want to hear the story of (Yitz'chak,) Isaac." He said, as He reached out to touch my hand.

"Do you mean the part where he was offered on the
altar?" I asked, already knowing the answer.
He nodded, then focused His eyes on the garment He was
awkwardly trying to fold. It never seemed to occur to Him that
men, or even boys for that matter, didn't help their mother's
unless it was absolutely necessary. I began to tell the tale…
"'Yitz'chak,'" Avraham walked over to his son and laid his hand on
his shoulder. "'The Lord *El Elohim*, Yahweh, has
asked me to worship him on top of Mount Moriah.
Please help the hired men prepare the wood
for the sacrifice.'"
"'Yea, Abba'."
Ever eager for an adventure, the sturdily built youth
leaped to his feet, and just for the sheer joy of it, jumped over a boulder
and wrestled with the exuberant big sheep *kelev* that was romping at
his heels.

"'Tie up the *kelev* before you go!'" Avraham called.

"Yitz'chak looked surprised. The dog always came wherever
they went, but did as he was told. *I suppose* Abba *is thinking
a lively kelev would disrupt the reverent atmosphere at a
sacrifice.* The dog's tail drooped in disappointment,
and he whined sadly after them.
"Soon, they were on their way. Yitz'chak reveled in the beauty of the
day. It was great going on a hike with his aged Abba and the hired
men, whom he had grown up with. Everything was so beautiful, from
the tiny flowers nestled between boulders to the fluffy clouds soaring
over-head.
"Yitz'chak was a joyful lad, he easily lived up to the
meaning of his name, which was *laughter'*
"'Abba, I saw a bear!'" Yitz'chak broke away from
the other climbers, and raced ahead.
"'Be careful son!'" Avraham tried to call out,
but the words shriveled on his tongue while his throat constricted.

"I was about to tell my son to be careful, yet I am thinking of slaying him! Can El' Elyon actually be asking that of me? Surely I must have misunderstood. It felt like his heart was splintering like shale.

"I never knew what it was to face such terrific agony before today. How **can** *I thrust a knife into my fine, strong dearly loved son's body? It has been so special watching him grow up. I feel like the worst sort of traitor! He's always loved and trusted me so much He has been the joy of my old age I am afraid Sarah suspected something because she seemed nervous and fidgety. Even Yitz'chak remarked about his mother's unhappiness.*

"'Mother, what are you so nervous about? I will be fine. I am not a baby any more, and besides, I have good people to protect me!'"

"Good people? Good people? To protect him?'
Hot tears squeezed out between
Avraham's eyelids as he plodded stolidly along.

"Surely, surely I must have misunderstood the Voice of El Elohim. I always believed He was a El Elohim of love and mercy!

"What will the Aleichem think if I sacrifice—if I make a— human—sacrifice—just—like they do? I have always spoken out against it. He stumbled over a rock, half-blinded by his tears, an elderly servant reached out to support his elbow.

"'Would you rest a while?'" he asked.
"'Nay, nay, I'll be fine.'"

"Can there be any good in what I am contemplating? Yitz'chak has been such an obedient boy. I know he will submit, he trusts me implicitly. Oh Yahweh, bear me up. I know it was El' Elyon speaking even though I am loath to admit it. I will obey. My heart is breaking but You mean more to me than anything else in this world. I'd rather have You than Yitz'chak even.

"The young men with the wood were striding a little ahead of Avraham, since he was plodding so slowly up the hill.

"Yitz'chak came scampering back, pausing for a moment to swing on a vine, and leap on to a mossy spot. Avraham almost smiled. *He reminds me so much of the frolicsome goats*
at this time. I have never seen him so vibrant
and full of life.
"His steps slowed. *Does he somehow sense these*
may well be his last days,
and he wants to enjoy them to the fullest?

"His servant was about to encourage him to stop once again when Yitz'chak's voice broke the high altitude stillness.

"'Gershom, I did see a bear!'" he called out
to one of the younger servants.
"'You should have come with me, watched it lope off into the woods.'"
"Then he stopped and grinned crookedly. Obviously, it would be too hard to be scrambling ahead with a load of wood strapped to one's back like Gershom had.

"All day long, Yitz'chak enjoyed the adventure, he was enthusiastically involved in setting up camp for the night, with the help of the two servants. It was exciting to get away from the docile sheep and sleepy cattle for a few days, to do something different!

"Yitz'chak hardly gave it a thought that they were going to a far distance place to make a sacrifice. Sacrifices were common occurrences during all his growing up years, it was just the distance they were traveling that was different.

"By the eighth hour of the third day, everyone's spirits were lagging, as well as their footsteps, and although Yitz'chak still frequently walked ahead, he wasn't as exuberant as he had been earlier in their journey.

"Today, as he ambled along, he would casually pluck off a flower now
and then, to examine its intricate beauty before tossing it aside.

"Avraham noticed that he still kicked at the rocks occasionally
but wasn't challenging the other men to see who could aim
better at a knot in a tree or some other such object.

Avraham was keenly aware that his son was becoming
more and more pensive.

"Does he know? Oh, HaShem, does he know what I am about to do?

"When Avraham lifted up his eyes and saw the place from afar, the
in his heart that he had thought could not get any worse, knifed
him anew. As they drew closer,
he quietly dismissed the young men, telling them that he
and Yitz'chak would go alone to worship and come again to them later.

"Yitz'chak's companions glanced at each other, then looked
down, but didn't say anything except to respectfully
agree to wait with the supplies.

Yitz'chak and
his father ascended together. They wouldn't have
considered questioning the elderly patriarch.

"He matched his pace to his father's. They walked in
companionable silence for a good half hour then *Yitz'chak*
squeezed out the words that had been on his mind all day.

"'My father, behold the fire and the wood, but
where is the lamb for the burnt offering?'"

"'My son, El Elohim will provide a lamb.'"

"Yitz'chak was fully aware that the heathen
offered human sacrifices, but would
his father do the same?

*"Surely, not! He is such a kindly old man, and he worships the El
Elohim of the universe, whom I had been taught is just and merciful.
Surely, Abba would not take my life! The life of his only son!*

"He felt his fists tighten but he had such deep respect for his father
that he couldn't allow himself to protest or voice his thoughts.
"Yet he loved life! As much if not more than many boys his age.
There was so much to see, to enjoy, to look forward to.
"He bit his lower lip, and cast a quick glance at his father. Earlier, his
Abba had seemed troubled, but now he was calm, almost resigned,
as if he really did believe that *El Elohim* would provide the lamb.

"The moment came all too soon. Yitz'chak forced
himself not to send his father reeling when the rope was
being wound around him a few minutes later.

Anger leaped into his heart. *My fist could flash out so
swiftly, he wouldn't even know what happened.*
"With more than human willpower, he quenched the
thought, but his eyes were glazed with pain.
"He stared at his father; he saw such faith and resignation on his dear
Abba's face that it seemed to seep into his own anguished soul.
*"I have a father like no other, if he loves El Elohim enough
to give me up, then I guess it will be worth sacrificing
my life in order to live with his El Elohim.*
"Yitz'chak kept his eyes fixed on his father's tender face, instead of
that awful blade, and refused to wonder if it would hurt very much.

The knife rose. Yitz'chak involuntarily gasped.
Suddenly, a powerful voice split the stillness.

"'Avraham*!* Avraham!'" Yitz'chak*'s* eyes popped open. "'Lay not thy
hand upon the lad, neither do anything unto him.'"

"His eyes widened. *That is the voice of the Lord
El Elohim! I have heard the voice of
the Adonai! It must be so!* Then into that breathless
stillness, the voice came once again.

"'Now I know that you fear *Adonai:* your Master, since
You have not withheld your son, your only son, from me.'"

"Avraham fumbled with the knots, it was hard to see them with all
the tears blurring his eyes. The two: young and old, father and son,
embraced for a very long time. They were too full of emotion to speak.
When Yitz'chak saw the ram caught in the thicket, he pointed silently.

"Yitz'chak watched humbly as the sheep gave up his life in his place.

"They both dropped to their knees in praise and
holy adoration to the One True *El Elohim.*

I, Mary'am, had been so caught up in the telling that I hadn't
noticed Yeshua wrapping His arms tightly around me.
He buried His head on my shoulder and had not stirred
once since pressing in close. Now, he looked up and I
saw that His dear, sweet face was tear-stained.

Why does this story affect him so, I agonized as I rested the
basket of wash on my hip and started the long climb up the
hill to the house. Yeshua pulled on my arm so I stopped.

"He didn't want to," He whispered, "He didn't want to make Avraham
suffer." He swallowed while I waited intently for Him to continue.
When he didn't immediately, I was distracted by a
swallow swooping and soaring over our heads. *We
had better hurry. It is beginning to cloud over.*

"Imma," he clutched at my sleeve. " He—the *HaShem*—
wants us to know how much it hurts---Him."

"W-what?" I stared at Him, all thoughts of swallows forgotten.
Yeshua seemed to be grasping something that I couldn't
comprehend, but for some reason it chilled my heart.

Marilyn Friesen

Nisan 27th

April 7th

DEAR DIARY,

All week long, I have been berating myself
because of our carelessness and neglect.

Because Yeshua has reached the all-important age of twelve, we took
Him along with us to the Passover in *Yerushalayim*. He has been
excitedly talking about it for weeks so we should have been warned.

Yeshua has always been a responsible lad, so we let Him wander
and talk with whom ever he would while we traveled.
I'm afraid we weren't as careful as we should have been. We
were delighted to meet with so many friends that we hadn't
seen in years, we were eager to catch up on their lives.

After we reached *Yerushalayim,* Yeshua went with his father to
have the lamb slain in the temple courtyard. I don't think Yeshua even
realized it, but Yosef told me much later that the lad had found it very
difficult to watch the lamb give his last gurgling breath.

As the sun was setting, Yeshua soberly turned the lamb while it was
being roasted on a rod of pomegranate wood. He didn't need
to, there were plenty of adults around, but He said,

"That's fine, I can do it."

His questions regarding the meaning of each separate part of the
paschal feast were more insightful than I have ever heard from anyone
before. He has amazingly deep thoughts for a twelve-year-old.

There were around fifteen of us feasting together, there was much
chatter and singing. I was enjoying the warm fellowship so thoroughly
that I was only dimly aware that Yeshua rarely smiled the whole evening.

I'm telling you this to show you that we should
have known where He would be.

But we were so happy to see friends and relatives
from far and near that we hadn't paid that much attention to what He
was doing. And besides, He is a responsible lad.

Well, when it was time to leave for Navara, we packed up and
sort of drifted along with the crowd heading north in the
general direction of Galilee, visiting as we went.

I guess we figured Yeshua had noticed us leave, that He
was tagging along behind with *yeled* His own age.
How foolish that was of us! Had we not realized how
eagerly He had participated in the discussions
in that special room in the temple?

He must have sat for hours on the mats with other boys
trying to learn from various religious leaders.
From time to time, other boys would pop up and run
out to play, but rarely could He be persuaded to leave,
continually sitting at the feet of a teacher.
Hadn't we also seen Him stop a *rebbe* on the street to ask Him
many questions about the true meaning of the Passover?
Had we not known that while on this trip, He rarely showed
interest in the games other boys were involved in?
Not a day had passed without Him spending at least some of His
time visiting with learned teachers and I know they
were impressed with his thoughtful insight.
I am wondering now if He was frightened when darkness fell,
since everyone had gone home and no one came to fetch Him.

Likely, someone offered Him a bed but He would
have declined saying, "Nay, my parents will be with
me shortly. I will stay here until they come."
He must have found a corner on a thin mat
somewhere, perhaps tucked his cloak around
Himself and slowly, lonesomely drifted off to sleep.

Perhaps he was thinking about the little boy, Samuel,
who also slept in the temple, wondering if the *HaShem*
would speak to Him also. Perhaps *Adonai* did.
Surely, oh surely, by the second night, someone would
have insisted that He come with them!
I hope someone gave Him something to eat.
Growing boys are always so hungry!

The next morning, when we still had not arrived, He most likely
was feeling famished and more than a little worried, but I am certain He
went back to the teachers and was soon involved in their discussions.
And to think that I reproved Him! Him! When it was our fault.
We should have known where He would be. The poor lad!
He must have been astonished that we hadn't looked in the temple
first, although I'm sure He must have spent at least some time
searching for us.

I still remember His pale disheveled appearance
and His meek response to my scolding.
"Whist ye not that I must be about my Father's
business?" He asked, rubbing tired eyes.
Ah, is He not too young to be taking His calling
so seriously? What manner of child is this?
We must watch over Him more carefully.
He could have been kidnapped if
the wrong people had caught on to who He really was!
Adonai, I am nephal!

19th Iyyar

April 29th

DEAR DIARY,

Someone told us that Yeshua was explaining things to the leaders while *they* asked *Him* questions! Can you grasp that?

I know we have a high regard for the inspirations of innocent children, but this goes far beyond that. A twelve-year-old instructing the teachers!

1st Cheshvan

October 17th

DEAR DIARY,

Zadok was over at the shop today. He is a handsome somewhat reckless youth close to Yeshua's age. It doesn't bother me if he comes when Yosef is around, but he seems to know when the boys' father is away from the shop and hangs around more often then.

I quickly poured a pitcher of cool water and filled a bowl with almonds and peach slices so they could refresh themselves.

Zadok had been speaking when I opened the door, but abruptly stopped. Our second son, Yaakov, had a look of rapt attentiveness on his face before he saw me. I wish he wasn't so interested in Zadok's defiant ways.

I very much like to see things from the other person's view point, however, so I will try and piece together what is happening from the bits and pieces Yeshua has shared with me over the last few months. Allow me to put it in story form so we can see it more clearly in our minds.

'I am so sick and tired of working in this old vineyard,' Zadok grumbled to his dog as he twined another vine around a support. 'Malachi always gets the better jobs. Abba knows how much I love to curry the horses, to exercise them, but nay, he must always leave the menial tasks for me and let Malachi do the more honorable work.' 'Where are the servants? They should have milked the cows and mucked out the barn long ago.'

He eyed the distance to the end of the row and then shook his head. *It's too hot to be working out here. I am going fishing. No one will notice if I'm gone for a few hours.*

Just then, he saw a couple servants with hoes over their shoulders ambling his way, he ducked behind some leafy vines. *I'll just cut across to the creek. They have enough help, now.* Zadok's thoughts were not much happier as he slouched on the brook bank even though the sun was soft against his skin, it dappled the grass and brook in patterns of light and darkness.

I'm sick and tired of living on this farm. It is so stagnant compared to city life. The boys in town invite me to go carousing with them but I have to sneak off because of all the work around here. Besides, Abba and Imma *have such an old fashioned attitude towards revelry.*

He brushed a lock of hair off his sweaty forehead and gently threw back the fish he had caught. *No use bringing any fish in for supper,* Imma *knows I am supposed to be in the vineyard.*

Why couldn't Abba have been a merchant, or a caravan driver or something like that? I'd leave tonight if I had the money.

He straightened his back as a new light came into his eyes. *I know what I'll do. I'll ask for my inheritance money. There is no need to wait until* Abba *dies to receive it. He might live to be three score and ten, if not more! I'll get it now.* And so that's why Zadok was shaking his head sadly, lamenting, "He wouldn't give it to me," when I brought them their refreshments.

11th Cheshvan

October 27th

DEAR DIARY,

Yeshua is quite concerned about Zadok. He says his discontentment
is increasing, he keeps pestering his father to give him the
inheritance money so he can strike out on his own. Naturally, his father
doesn't think he is mature enough to handle that great a sum of money,
but Zadok won't give in easily. He never does.
Zadok's father has even switched the boys' jobs in order to make
him happier. Now Malachi is the one that spends long hours doing
field and similar types of work, I haven't heard any rumors
that he complains. Of course, Zadok still has to help him.

Zadok is caring for those horses that he loves, but
I wonder if *Hezekiah* will ever regret
getting them? Our religious leaders do not support us owning horses
to breed with donkeys, even when raised to sell to Gentiles. Hopefully,
Zadok will be more contented now that he is responsible for their care.
I can imagine how burdened *Hezekiah* and Martha must feel. It is a
grievous thing when children rebel against concerned parents.

27th Iyyar

May 7th

DEAR DIARY,

Our Lydia is growing up so quickly, no, but unfortunately she is most
unladylike. Sometimes I am bewildered how to prepare her for her
future role as a wife and mother which is coming up so fast,

Whenever possible, she is out with her brothers and their friends
showing off her ability with the sling shot, or competing to scramble up
the highest tree. Some of the lads are impressed, but Yaakov, especially,
gets pretty disgusted with her and call her an *Ayopokoitoo*: (tomboy).

Yeshua, who is usually so patient, advises her to go home and attend
to her duties, which she most emphatically does not want to do!

One day, she was scampering around like a kid, or should
I say like one of those monkeys that the Egyptians like
to own as pets. That would be more accurate.

She had been making her way up a tree on one of the numerous
hills surrounding our town. In her effort to climb faster and higher
than her brothers, she snagged her dress when a branch broke.
Fortunately, it slowed her fall considerably, but
there was a dreadful rip in the material.

It was an old dress that was already turning a dingy gray
from many trips to the creek bank, but I thought it would
teach her some responsibility if she had to mend it.
Knowing our little *Ayopokoitoo* the way I do, I wasn't a bit
surprised when she pouted at first, but then her face lit up.

"Imma," she cried, "since I made such a nasty three-cornered tear in
the fabric, and the edges are kind of frayed anyway, may I patch it?"

Marilyn Friesen

"Yea, *tinoki*."
She came up close to me with the garment
held eagerly in her hands.
"Imma," she begged, "you know, I never did like this boring
material. May I use a leftover scrap from my new Shabbat day robe to
mend it?"
"That will not work, because your Shabbat material has never
been washed. It will shrink and cause trouble."

"Just let me try, Imma, please. I will sew very carefully. I will show
you that I can! That rose color would look so pretty against the gray."
I had to admit that it would be attractive, albeit, somewhat incongruous.
"I was about to remind her that the rent would be made
worse, but she can be such a willful *riba*. Sometimes, it is best to learn
the hard way, I reasoned. "Do what pleases you, yea."
"Oh, thank you, thank you, Imma!" she cried, giving me a hug. I
went back to my own mending but watched as she eagerly cut out a
piece of rose-colored material and carefully basted it before sewing it
on to the torn garment. When I saw how uncharacteristically
careful she was being, I felt a twinge of guilt..
Yaakov and Jose were sitting nearby, Yeshua was helping
them memorize Hebrew scripture in a low chant.
Yeshua studied Lydia with a bemused expression on his face, and
then He glanced at me with a slight smile.
I think He knew perfectly well
what I was trying to teach His younger sister.

Sure enough, the next time she scrubbed the robe over the rocks
and it dried, she found out that the patch had started to shrink and
fray in a most unattractive manner. I'd like to say that she learned
her lesson completely and was always obedient after that, but
life is not quite that easy. She did, however, learn to ask me if any
piece of material she chose would be *suitable* to use for mending.

11ᵗʰ Tammuz

June 19ᵗʰ

DEAR DIARY,

Zadok has disappeared! Everyone in our small village is at their wit's end! Where could the son of the richest man in the neighborhood be? Upon closer investigation, they discovered that a fine young stallion is missing also, so no one really suspects kidnapping. It's sad to think that Zadok may have run away.

12ᵗʰ Tammuz

June 20ᵗʰ

DEAR DIARY,

Yeshua found out from Malachi that Zadok received his inheritance from his father last night. He was not at all surprised that Zadok is gone. I saw Malachi leave the yard I and have never seen him looking so, troubled is not the right word; he seems so gloomy since his brother has gone missing. I wonder what is going through the dear boy's, I mean young man's, mind?

DEAR DIARY,

We once had a neighbor who was so burdened. Yeshua became good friends with her son, *Aram,* soon after we returned from Egypt.

As a matter of fact, the two boys could play all day long with hardly a quarrel. I did not get to know *Tamar* very well at the time because she was a quiet, retiring sort of person who didn't come out very often. But something happened to change all that.

When the boys were both eight-years-old, Aram's father went on a trip to Jericho. He had to pick up something for his master and was in a hurry to get back home so pressed on even after nightfall, instead of stopping at a *khan.* Of course the inevitable happened, he was attacked by thieves. After beating him viciously, they stripped him of most of his raiment and all of his money, as well as the parcel he was carrying. It was high noon the next day before anyone paused to help.

By then, he was raging with fever, he kept muttering something about a priest and a Levite passing by without stopping to help him. The man who finally did give him *tzedakah* (aid) was a Samaritan, may *El Elohim*'s blessings rest upon him. He offered him a drink from his flask, he could barely swallow water, then managed to get him up on his donkey. Sadly, the poor man expired; he had no next of kin, other than his distraught widow and their son.

Tamar has never been the same since. It wounded her deeply knowing that no one had stopped to help him earlier, lest he might still be among the living. Alas, too soon that was almost the least of her troubles.

The coffin had just been lowered into the ground and
the mourners were going their respective ways.
Suddenly, a very haughty-looking
man dressed in the finest of raiment stepped up to
her. I saw this happen with my own eyes.
"Sorry to bother you at such a difficult time," he said,
"but your rent is past due, I was wondering
when you would be able to pay it?"
"Overdue?" Tamar gasped. "But I thought my husband always paid
it promptly on the first of the month!"

"It is very unfortunate that he has deceived you, but he has not paid me for the last three months, something must be done about it now."

I saw Yosef's jaws tighten, I wasn't surprised when he stepped
forward to lay a restraining hand on the man's shoulder.
"Excuse me, sir. It is most inappropriate to discuss business matters at a funeral. You should give her at least a few days of grace. She is still
reeling from shock."
Three pairs of eyes were fixed on Yosef. The landlord's
eyes were fiery, the poor widow's eyes were warm with
gratitude, of course mine shone with pride.
It did not look like the landlord was going to back down easily
so Yosef motioned for me to take Tamar home with me.

A rather heated, though mostly one-sided, discussion assailed our ears as we walked away. Moments later, the landlord strode after us, pulled at Tamar's sleeve and continued demanding money.

It is most inappropriate for a man to touch a woman and we were scandalized at that, but what was worse was his persistence.

Finally, Tamar sighed wearily, and said she would see if she had enough money on hand for one month's rent but she wasn't sure what they would live on. He almost groveled in his apparent gratitude but that didn't cause us to trust him one bit more.

10th Adar

February 20th

DEAR DIARY,

In the next few months, we became heartbreakingly
aware that things were going hard for Tamar.
Even poor little Aram lost his infectious grin.

Several of us from the synagogue would slip over to her place from
time to time with a little baking, a few eggs from our flocks, or fresh
vegetables; which is the *tzedakah*, (merciful, just) thing to do. Eventually,
she had to move into a dreadful tenement building in the city and
find work. She could not afford to pay the so-called *unpaid* rent.

The man found her new address and kept hounding her. What
really broke my heart, and made our children whimper long into
the night, was when I found out that she had sold her son, her own,
dear, precious *yeled*, into slavery in order to appease the scoundrel.

Nothing so awful has happened in our neighbourhood before;
although I sadly admit it is common enough among the gentiles.

28th Adar

March 10th

DEAR DIARY,

"Imma," Lydia once asked, wrapping her arms around herself as if to keep warm, "will we ever get so poor that you would sell us into slavery?"

Yaakov sat up straight and stopped what he was doing.

His younger brothers stopped tussling
on the floor and stared at me.
"Never, my dear," I answered with a warm smile.
"But what if Abba would die or something," Jose's eyes were
round with worry, Shimon looked about ready to cry
so I scooped him up onto my lap.
"Jehovah would help us."
"But He didn't help Aram!" Jose protested.
I reached out to put my arm around his shoulder.
For once, he didn't squirm away.
"We must trust. I know *HaShem* will watch over us. Even
though we can't tell, I know He is watching over Aram and
his mother."

The children nodded soberly, although they didn't
argue, I could see that they were not satisfied.

"Believe what Imma says," Yeshua encouraged
gently. *"As a Father comforts
his children so will I comfort you,* saith the Lord."

I saw Yosef cast Him a grateful smile but I wondered
why he hadn't participated in the discussion.

I rose, holding the garment I had just finished in
my uplifted hands. Shimon slid off my lap.
"Here Lydia," I said, "your cloak is done, try it on." As I helped her
get her arms into the dolman sleeves, she wriggled in anticipation.
"It's perfect, Imma, so warm and cozy." She snuggled down
on the sheep fleece which was spread out on her pallet.

"It's perfect," she said once again, popping up. She slid her arms
out of the sleeves and pulled the hood around her face so the cloak
would wrap her like a blanket. "I could go to sleep right now."
"…even before supper?" Yeshua asked drolly.
"Nay, not I!" She leaped to her feet and thrust her arms
back in the sleeves before twirling around the room.
We had to flatten ourselves against the walls
to keep from getting bumped, but
fortunately her antics didn't last long.

After the children had gone to bed, I tucked Lydia's feet in at
the bottom of her thick new robe, which was so much longer
than the one she had outgrown, and I knelt beside her.

"Lydia, try to think of *HaShem* every time
you wear this warm new robe."
By the light of the candle in my hand, I saw her looking
at me expectantly. Her gaze was so sweet, so eager.
"*HaShem*," I said softly, reverently, "wants to surround you with
His love and care, just like this cloak surrounds you.
She flung her arms around me. "I will Imma, I will, and even
if I'm sold into slavery, like Naaman's little maid, I'll take this
cloak with me to remind me of His care— yours too!"
I shuddered slightly and drew my fingers along her cheekbone.

Please *El Shaddai*, take care of my little lambs, I beg you!

19th Nisan

March 30th

DEAR DIARY,

Since Tamar moved away, we have not heard from her directly, but her name and *Aram's* are often mentioned in our family prayers. Oh, the poor destitute widow. What will happen to her?

24th Nisan

April 4th

DEAR DIARY,

We haven't heard anything about Zadok for many months now,
either, but I often wonder how he is doing. His parents must be
anguished because of the choices he's making.
We pray almost daily that he can find his way back to the
faith of his youth and be reconciled with his parents.
Malachi, the other son, has the reputation
of being a righteous hard worker.
That must be a comfort to Hezekiah and Martha, although
there is something about the lad's attitude that doesn't seem
quite right. Why does there have to be so much heartache in
the world? I am sure *El Shaddai* does not want it that way

DEAR DIARY,

The sun is deep into the hills and I really should
be getting the goat's milk strained. Lydia has just brought it in,
but I have something important to write about first.

We heard that dear timid Tamar was so desperate, she
went to a judge. When he didn't take her seriously, she
was even brave enough to find out where he lived.

The poor lady hounded him day after day, even late
in the evenings, asking him to please look into her
situation and see what he could do to help her.
Someone told us they had seen him duck
behind a pillar or into a shop, on more than one occasion,
when he saw her coming. What a cold-hearted man!
Finally, he investigated her situation because he was sick
and tired of seeing her tear-stained pleading face.
None of her former *Aleichem* were a bit surprised to find
out that her husband had not owed that landlord anything.
Even more appalling, this awful landlord had gradually
more than doubled the rent because he knew how ignorant the young
widow was concerning business matters, and he knew she could not read.

I am thrilled to say that Aram was speedily returned to
his mother, they are back in Navara once again.
The villagers welcomed her with open arms; it took a while, but
she seems more happy and secure than in former years. I think it
helped her to trust in Jehovah more. *Amen Alleluia El ohim!*

Oh, and one more wonderful bit of news, she has had the opportunity to wed a kindly man whose wife passed away in childbirth this year previous. I'm sure she will accept and gladly mother his three little ones; they are all younger than *Aram*.

I hope it is not wicked of me to be glad about it, but her landlord has to *pay* her rent for the next five years.

I must run and care for the milk.

27th Adar

March 9th

DEAR DIARY,

I hope it won't strain your memory, my dear diary, if I refer to Shoshoni, my childhood friend, but try to recall that she was the daughter of a merchant.

Remember how I told you that Yeshua and I sat beside her the first time we came to synagogue, after our return from Egypt?

I have a morsel of news I would like to share with you. Since she was an only child, her father took her husband into the business with him, but that isn't the real significant news.

I'll get to that yet. Navara was all astir recently with the news that a huge pearl had been discovered in a nearby field. I wonder what king might have had it hidden there perhaps during a fateful war? When Shoshoni's father found it there, he sold everything, yea, everything he owned, to buy the field where he had found the pearl!

Now, after bringing the pearl to the moneychangers, having received in exchange many sacks full of coin, the whole clan is moving to Alexandria where they are likely to prosper mightily.

Naturally, some of our boys and their friends armed themselves with picks and shovels and are scouring that area for more hidden treasure.

Yeshua looked thoughtful when he heard the story
of the lost pearl, so I sat down beside him.
The late afternoon sun slanted across his face
as we sat and conversed. It brought to mind the
wonderful *Shekinah* of the Holy One because the glory
seemed to come from within and without.

"Would to *HaShem* that people would be willing to sell all
that they have for the Pearl of Great Price," He remarked.
He rose as if to go, I laid my hand on His arm.
"What is the pearl of great price?"
He gazed thoughtfully into my eyes.
"The kingdom of heaven."
He could see that I was puzzled, so He continued.
"If men would be willing to give up all that they
have in the world *El'Elohim* would
bestow the *banoah* of Heaven on them which is worth far more."

December 17th

DEAR DIARY,

Dear Yosef and Mary'am, *(This is the letter that I later wrote in my mind to fill in the details of this incident; the real letter is further on. I guess I still have that youthful silliness that likes to add all kinds of unnecessary details to my journals!)*

We are in quite a bind. I, Gideon, fell, and broke my leg, all of my heavy work has fallen on Rachael and my wife's slender shoulders.

I had been searching for one of the ewes that had gone astray. We think she was hiding while giving birth, but it may be that in her bulky condition she lay down somewhere and cannot get up.

While I was gone, a sudden rain storm, a deluge actually, came up, I was desperate to find the ewe before she died. Since I had been mucking along in the storm and it was dark, I didn't realize the edge of an embankment was so near until the ground gave way beneath my feet. I tumbled towards the ravine.

The stream had overflowed as usual but my foot was caught—it twisted in a root which fortunately saved me from drowning. I managed to edge up back to solid ground, but I was in so much pain. In the driving rain, it was impossible to limp back home.

When Rachael, after much searching, managed to find me, she took my dagger and whacked off a stout branch which I then used for a crutch. My leg is broken so I will be laid up for more than a day or two.

Rachael is looking after the rest of the sheep but I need someone to find the lost one because she is one of my best ewes.

May *El Shaddai* have pity and restore her to good health.

Some of the neighbor boys, on whom we would have depended upon in the past, have been hanging around with the Zealots, sneaking off to their meetings. So they care not to come to our aid. I hope they will get over this fanatical notion soon, it is so dangerous. Nevertheless, we are in serious trouble.

Could Yeshua come?

This is what Gideon really wrote. He is a man of few words, fewer yet in writing.

Could you spare Yeshua for a few days?
I lost an ewe and busted my leg.
Gideon

Yeshua rolled up the scroll He had been studying and rose to His feet. "If it is alright with you, Abba and Imma, I am ready and willing to go."

I could tell that Yosef was thinking about the window lattices Yeshua was working on for a priest's new house. He sighed and said, "Go, son. If that is Your desire, You are excused from Your duties here at home."

"Thank you, Abba. I believe I will go right away so that I can get there before dark. Do you mind if I take the donkey?"

"That would be expected." Yosef ran his hand through his hair and frowned slightly. Then he jumped up and hurried to the shop. I knew that our newly imported religious leader was an exacting demanding customer and Yosef felt he would have to put aside his other work to finish the project himself.

5th Tevet

December 18th

DEAR DIARY,

After visiting with Yeshua when He returned, this is pretty much
how I picture the happenings of the last few
days. Sorry, my imagination is
running wild once again.

As Yeshua hurried down the long dusty road, warm memories of
carefree hours spent on Gideon's farm filled His mind. The house
came into view and He debated whether he should go straight to Rachael
to check on the flock, or see how the man of the house was doing.

It wasn't a hard decision, however. People came first with Yeshua.
My cousin, Salome, scurried to the door when He arrived.

"Yeshua, I am so glad you came! We were expecting a
message telling us when you would be able to get away,
but here You are in person."
Yeshua smiled. "How is Dohd Gideon doing?"
"Miserable and cranky," she grinned, "he's really chafing about
having to stay put on such a bright sunny day."
Her face clouded. "It would be a miracle if that ewe actually
survived the night. Do hurry and see if you can find her!"
"Is that Yeshua's voice I hear?"
"It is I, Gideon." Yeshua went over to the sleeping bench where
Gideon was lying and looked at him compassionately.
"I hope you will soon be well."

"I do, too," Gideon grunted. "A rather youthful upstart by the
name of Luke set it, using comfrey and other stuff, I think.
It seems to be healing okay even if he was a Greek."

Gideon told Yeshua in detail where the ewe
had strayed away from the flock.

Just as Yeshua turned to leave, Gideon reached out and
squeezed his hand. "We appreciate this. We considered hiring
someone from the village to help us, but hirelings
really do not care whether or not a dumb sheep is rescued,
especially if they have to get wet and dirty searching for it."

I suppose Yeshua nodded sympathetically, knowing full well what a
soft spot Gideon had for each one of his sheep. He could call them
each by name and they would come running.
He treated them more like pets than livestock.

"My staff is in the corner by the door," he called as Yeshua headed out.
"Taudi !"

Salome hurried after Him with a small lunch and a wineskin
full of water. With a genial wave of his hand, Yeshua was off.
I imagine Salome gazing through the open door long after
He was but a dot on the horizon. I know I would have.

In spite of all the mud, it did not take Yeshua long to catch sight of
Rachael. She was perched on a boulder, her long hair was flying around
her. He heard the sound of her harp floating on the air even before He
caught sight of her, thinking that nothing could be more
heavenly than that sweet music on a perfect summer's day.

If it wasn't for the wet grass slapping his ankles, almost up to
His knees, He wouldn't have believed there had been such a
fierce storm during the night, it was so bright and clear.

Rachael was glad to see him,
but they did not talk long. It was imperative that Yeshua
get to the more rugged terrain before darkness set in.

I imagine that Yeshua sang the psalm Rachael had been strumming as He jogged across the field towards the ravine where Gideon had fallen,. He loves to sing.

He told me later that as He neared the more wooded area, closer to the streambed, a few birds flitted in and out of the trees. He paused to listen to, them, imitating the sounds of the ones nearest Him. Soon, a flock of chirping birds had swarmed closer, one even landed on His arm and another on His shoulder.

I can picture Him stroking them gently before they flew off to a nearby branch, watching Him expectantly with their bright beady eyes in their tiny tilted heads. Yeshua carefully broke off a piece of the loaf of bread Salome had provided and scattered the crumbs at His feet. A dozen or so variously hued birds materialized from the leafy branches nearby and gathered for the unexpected snack.

They didn't seem very hungry, however, possibly because worms and other insects were in abundance since the recent downpour. Yeshua soon went on His way.

One barely feathered-out sparrow didn't make it to the banquet. It sort of tumbled out of its nest and started to soar erratically before plunging to the ground. Yeshua knelt down and picked it up but there was no fluttering heartbeat.

"Poor little fledging," he probably murmured, then scooped some dirt and leaves from beneath a tree so He could cover the bird with plenty of leaves and twigs. Its parents hovered anxiously around until Yeshua rose to His feet and brushed off His robe, then they flew away.

Once again, Yeshua would have reminded Himself that He did not have time to linger so He walked in a zigzag path, with His head down, as He searched for any sign of the sheep's trail.

This proved to be quite difficult because its tracks
had been washed away. Eventually,
He came across trampled areas in the grass which may have
indicated where the flock had been. He carefully circled
the area for any sign of one ewe's meandering ways.

After many false starts, Yeshua found what He was pretty
certain was the correct path, following it carefully.

Yeshua was able to go at a fairly good pace because of the staff's aid,
but I bet He kept looking at the sky because the sun had reached
its zenith long before, it was rapidly descending.

I'm sure He called from time to time but wondered if the sheep
would give an answering bleat if it did not recognize His voice;
that would be a needless worry. Of course they knew His voice!

Much later, while we were reminiscing one evening, Yeshua told me how
much that reminded Him of His Heavenly Father's sheep, those who
refuse to answer when they are called. He sounded so sad at the time.

He longs to be a good shepherd when that responsibility is laid on
His shoulders. Yeshua cares so much for all of *El Shaddai*'s helpless
sheep, especially those who are alone and frightened.

I strayed from my story, yes? After a while, Yeshua heard a matronly
baa. He listened carefully to ascertain from whence it came.
Yeshua carefully climbed down a rocky mountain slope when
He glimpsed the tangled wool of a sheep. He hooked His
staff around the sheep's belly, then gently pulled it
to a flat grassy spot on the top of the hill.

I wondered why she hadn't bothered to climb up herself. I was
familiar with the area and knew it wasn't all that steep.

To His surprise, the sheep resisted His efforts to be lifted up,
on closer investigation, He understood why. On a nearby ledge
sheltered by a slight overhang, He noticed a feeble newborn
lamb. He crawled slowly towards it, being careful not to dislodge
any rocks, while talking softly to the distressed sheep.

Using His staff and His hands, He was able to lift the lamb
over the top. The sheep just lay where He had placed it, sides
heaving, its listless brown eyes watching His every
move.

Yeshua was dismayed when He saw, just a short while later, that
the lamb appeared to be dead. He laid it beside its Imma anyway.
She closed her eyes and seemed to lose interest, now that her
baby had been rescued. Yeshua crouched beside the ewe,
encouraging her to smell her little lamb, then He picked
it up and cradled it in His arms, sorrowing.

The trees in the distance had become black silhouettes but Yeshua was
reluctant to give up on the seemingly lifeless lamb. As He held it close
to His warmly-beating heart, tucked inside His cloak, Yeshua thought,

*Oh if people could only grasp how concerned the Heavenly
Father is when His human sheep are not doing well.* He
sighed, pressing the little face against His cheek.

Unexpectedly, the ewe struggled to her feet and started nosing her
baby. Yeshua found her actions intriguing, so He pushed the limp
creature closer to its mother while she bleated softly and nuzzled it.

Under Yeshua's searching, sensitive fingers, He felt a little movement;
the slightest twitch it was, as He exclaimed with joy, "This lamb
is not dead after all. Thank You, thank You, my Father!"

Since Yeshua is a tender-hearted lad, I suppose tears moistened
His eyes, tears of pure relief. After the lamb uttered a

feeble bleat, Yeshua positioned it beside the mother so that
it could receive some rich life-giving nourishment.
By then, the sun was dying in the west, the
first star was out. Yeshua lay on the cool grass with
the lamb sheltered between Him and the ewe.
He tucked His cloak around Himself and the tiny shivering newborn.
I am sure He did not mind that it was cold and uncomfortable
out there in the wilderness. All that He was really concerned
about was that the poor frightened, although disobedient, sheep
had been rescued, and her little one's life had been saved.
Gideon's sheep know they are supposed to come when they are
called, that's why I call it disobedient. The ewe would have been so
much safer had she only listened.

Yeshua chose to spend the night on the mountainside instead of taking
the risk of getting lost on such rugged terrain. Perhaps the ewe
wondered why it could not return home immediately. I know not if
ewes can think, but Yeshua knew that the way back was long and
hard; it would be better to travel when there was better light.

The sky was stained with the rosy pink glow of sunrise when Yeshua
checked the Imma sheep once more for injuries, removed a few burrs,
and then hoisted the tiny, now active, baby lamb to His shoulders.

I'm sure a wide grin split Yeshua's face and His steps
quickened when He caught sight of the mud-brick
house located just outside of the small hamlet.

Soon, His voice lifted up in the words of a psalm because He just
could not contain His joy, His voice drifted over the meadows.

"Im!" Rachael called, "Yeshua is coming back." They
all came running out to meet Him, while Gideon
hollered impatiently from his sleeping couch.

"Rejoice with me for I have found the sheep which was lost," Yeshua called. When He got closer, He added, "and there is a lamb also."

Rachael could not contain herself. She danced with joy while the rest, including the servants, expressed their gratitude in various ways.

Salome hurried in to show the wee creature to Gideon; he fondled it affectionately and called it Storm.

Later, Yeshua told me in a low voice, "If only *Yahweh's* children could know how happy He is when they return to their Father."

DEAR DIARY,

We received word from a spice trader that Zadok is in Gaza, faring sumptuously. Not so long ago, he was seen in Lachish. I wonder if he is heading to the sea, and how far he will go. If only he would invest his money in something practical, even if he chooses not to follow the Holy One, hallowed be His Name. Soon, his money will have been it will be all squandered, he will be destitute!

I have heard that Hezekiah bitterly regrets investing in horses. "It's not that horses are so wrong," Yosef explained to us, "they have been permitted since Solomon's time, but the way he uses some of them is unacceptable."

He told me in private that Hezekiah has been breeding certain ones with donkeys to produce mules, against the advice of the priest. He sadly complains that Zadok mightn't have been so bold about getting away if he hadn't had his own fine thoroughbred. But I'm sure if Zadok was determined enough he would have eventually left anyway

DEAR DIARY,

Hezekiah has lost all interest in raising animals for breeding purposes. He has sold most of them and has put in more crops this fall.

It was a *banoah* to hear that his heartbreak has helped him to be more charitable to the poor. According to Yeshua, Hezekiah was short of workers during harvest time so he went to the marketplace several times a day to look for help.

He actually paid those that came at the eleventh hour the same wage as those that bore the heat and discomfort of the whole day! How considerate of him, some of those fellows have been desperate for work far too long.

27th Adar

March 9th

DEAR DIARY,

I was sweeping the floor in the shop today when Yeshua's former classmate, Amos, burst in.
His face was mottled and red, his fists clenched against his sides.
"I'm furious!" he shouted.
Yeshua rested his hand on the beam he was about to saw and looked up; Yosef stopped riveting a cart wheel. I leaned on my broom handle and gazed at him. Yeshua's pet dove cooed once, then was silent.

"I'm furious!" he repeated, as if we hadn't heard him the first time, stomping his foot on the ground for emphasis.
"What is the matter, son?" Yosef asked gently.

"An enemy sowed tares in our field. I don't know how he got away with it, without the dogs barking, but he did. He did! He must have come several nights in a row to do so much damage."
He slammed his fist against the rough -hewn wall
of the shop, I pitied him when he winced.
"Why do you think he did it?" I asked.
"I don't know, but I'm aiming to find out! Our crop is ruined, ruined entirely. We could never weed them out without destroying the wheat, they look too much alike."
"What does your Abba say?" Yeshua asked.
"Just leave them. We'll sort them out at harvest."

"Wasn't he angry?" Yaakov inquired.

Amos shook his head. "You know Abba, so easy going. I don't know why anyone would ever pick on him."
"Someone is jealous, yes?"

Marilyn Friesen

Amos' eyes widened. "Jealous? Hear ye, you may be right!
Some of the farmers complain that Abba's
crops are so much better than theirs.
"Lots of people stop in here. I want you to let
me know if you hear who did it."

"You know we won't do that, Amos..." Yosef started
to say, the angry youth stormed out and slammed the
door before Yosef could finish his comment.

We all stood and stared at each other. *Why would anyone do such
a mean thing?* While we thoughtfully discussed the situation, it didn't
feel like such a perfectly balmy early spring morning after all.

We had scarcely gotten back to work when
the door was pushed open again.
"Was Amos in here?" inquired the boy's father. We nodded.
"If he comes in again, you reason with him, yes? I'm
afraid for what he might do in a fit of temper."

Yosef put his hand on the other man's shoulder.
"What do you think caused the problem?"
"It started a couple years back, I'm afraid.
That is, if it is who I think it is."
We all waited for him to continue. I brushed a fly away from my face.
"Jonas has land adjoining mine, to the south. A herd of wild asses
came through and were destroying his crop. Jonas called on a few
men and boys to help. They chased off the asses but, how do you
say it? The boys got too rowdy, Amos was their ringleader.

They trampled more of the corn than was necessary."
Just then, we heard Jude shouting rather boisterously
to some of the boys he was playing ball with,
Yosef and I exchanged slightly amused but knowing looks.

"Wild asses can be pretty obstinate, though." Yeshua asserted.

Amos' father, David, agreed with a sigh.
"Jonas has been pretty testy ever since,
but then last year our sheep
got into his field. It should have never happened, but Amos' brother,
Benjamin, fell asleep while watching them, and well . . .
this looks like revenge."
"It might not have been Jonas."
"Nay, but he does have cause. "Amos' father stroked his beard
thoughtfully.

"If you get your hands on our boy, try to calm him
down, yes?" His glance strayed over to Yeshua, and he added, "If you
can spare your boys at harvest, it would sure be appreciated. Separating
the darnel from the wheat one stalk at a time will slow us down, no?"

After he left, I continued with my sweeping, Yosef with his
tacking, but Yeshua stared at the door for a moment.

"I just thought of something," he said in a low voice. We both
stopped to listen.

"We are like wheat and tares. On the outside, we are all
pretty much the same. Most people are just average,
they don't get angry unless
provoked; they don't lie and steal . . . very much. But *HaShem* knows
our hearts. He knows who is like darnel and
who is like wheat on the inside."
It looked like He wanted to say more, we waited
for Him to continue, but He didn't.

That night, I found Him wandering outside looking at the stars after
everyone else was asleep. I softly called from a distance so as not
to startle Him. When He turned toward me, I was the
one that was startled. He had tears in his eyes!

"Mind if I talk to you, Imma?"

"Gladly."

An older child never knows how eagerly a mother waits to hear those words. He led me up the ladder to the rooftop, we each found a mat to drop down on and rest. I leaned forward slightly, eager to know what was on His mind.

Wispy clouds were gathering, playing chase
with a thin crescent of a moon.

"Remember what I said about the tares, Imma?"

I nodded.

"I said only *HaShem* could discern between the tares and the wheat."

I agreed. He looked down at His scarred
carpenter's hands before continuing.

"Ye are all tares." My eyes widened but I didn't protest.
I knew He wasn't being disrespectful. Even in the semi-
darkness, I could see that He was troubled.

"No one is righteous enough to be anything but *tares*. Nay, not one."

He lowered His head into His hands, completely concealing
His soft youthful beard for a moment, and then looked up.

"Imma, it takes a miracle of *HaShem* to change darnel
into wheat. There is power in the blood."

I had no idea what He meant but it sent a thrill of apprehension
down my back and I sure wasn't going to ask.

When a chill wind came up, we went back
down the ladder. We were subdued.

DEAR DIARY,

Yaakov, he is becoming a problem, yes? He influences
his younger brethren to be unruly also.

I was walking over to the adjoining carpenter shop to tell them that the
evening meal was prepared when I heard Yaakov's sharp agitated voice.
"That Jonas, he is becoming as boastful as a cock."
Where is Yosef *that he did not reprove the boy?* My steps
slowed, not that I meant to listen to what was not for
my ears, but it just happened unconsciously.
"Remember how he sowed tares in David's field?"
"That was never proven…" that was Yeshua's calm steady voice
resonating against the background staccato of a hammer.
"Now he," Yaakov interrupted, "Jonas I mean, has the finest
crop in the country. He is boastful, yes? Even his son, little
Samuel, struts around with his chest puffed out like a cock."
"It is an excellent crop." I opened the door while Yeshua was speaking.
"Shalom, Imma," the boys chorused, then Jose
continued in a loud excited voice,
"He has started to dismantle his barns in order to build
a larger one. He will be adding field to field, next. He
will end up destroying ancient landmarks!"
"Does he not work too hard as it is?" I went over to stroke
the dove's silky feathers, "His small boy rarely sees him."
"Money is his *El Elohim*," Yaakov sneered. Jude
nodded vigorously and nudged Jose.
Yeshua bit His lip thoughtfully. "It appears to be so."
"Where is Abba?" I asked, changing the subject.
"An errand boy came," Jose replied, ""he seemed to be in a great
rush. Abba went with him. He said to eat without us."

The children were probably as talkative as usual during our evening meal, but I was feeling apprehensive, yet I knew not why.

When it was time to snuff out the candles and go
to bed my daughters sensed my uneasiness.

"Where's Abba, Imma?" Ruthalei asked, tugging at my hand. I sat down on a stool, rocking her in my arms. "He was called away. He will come back as soon as possible."

"But it's dark time, Imma. He didn't sing a psalm,
or pray with us." "Yeshua did, remember?"
"Yeshua's good, I like my big brother." She hopped off my lap and headed for her pallet. It was dark in her little corner of the room.
"You will tuck me in, yes?"
"Yea, *tinoki.*"
I brought the lamp over to her pallet and tucked
the covers snuggly around her small frame.

Thanks to the kindly shepherds from Beth Lechem, new woolly sheepskins were delivered from time to time by caravan to cover our children with. They also deliver us news from my *chavivi* back in Beth Lechem. This is their way of showing gratitude for being able to worship the newborn King. Because of the sheep skins, our children are warmer and more comfortable at night than many of their friends, but we don't want them to boast about it.
Shortly afterwards, I drifted off to sleep but I awakened when I felt a gentle touch on my shoulder.
I turned and reached out sleepily to Yosef.
"Mary'am, get up quietly. Suzanna needs
you." Instantly, I was wide awake.
"Is it Jonas?" Suzanna was Jonas' wife.
"Yea."
Yosef handed me my dress, it was on a hook beside the bed. I groped my way into it by the meager light of the moon.

"Imma!" Ruthalei called out in her sleep. I laid my
hand gently on her shoulder until she settled.
We crept silently into the night, then walked briskly through the
village streets to Jonas' house on the outskirts. The windows were
yellow with candlelight, which wasn't a good sign at such a late hour.

The same messenger boy that had summoned
Yosef earlier came to the door.
When Suzanna saw me,
she flung her arms around me and started to weep.
Jonas lay there so still and waxen-featured that I avoided looking
at him. Suzanna clung to me, I cradled her in my arms.
"Were there any last words?" I heard Yosef ask Yisrael, Jonas's father.
"He looked at Suzanna," Yisrael, replied,
"and then he looked at me. He uttered one word,
"*Niphal*", sorry,' then his eyes closed."
"It is enough, no?" Yosef asked.
Yisrael shrugged his shoulders and looked down. "We know not."

I bit my lip, *Sheol, the place of the dead, is an unwelcome place.*

Dawn was pinking the eastern sky, the yard was filling with hired
mourners. I wanted to leave, but Suzanna was clinging to me as if I was
her mother, so I thought needed to stay.
We knew that the younger children would be in good hands with
Yeshua there, but as the long day slowly wore
on, I longed to be with them.

Many people came and went.

It was hard not to look at the partially dismantled barn in the distance.
Aleichem came and finished harvesting for Suzanna, but I think she
hardly noticed. She would have rather had Jonas back than all that
surplus grain. Suzanna was distraught with grief. I spent as much
time as possible with her, as did others. Her own parents were dead.

The sudden tragedy cast a somber pall over the community and in my heart in particular. I have known for several years that Yosef had heart trouble and was tiring more quickly with each passing year. Death comes in threes. The old superstition clenched at my stomach, but I tried to ignore it.

22nd Tevet

January 12th

DEAR DIARY,

Only three weeks have passed and the Death Angel has come once again. Surely, surely, he will be satisfied now! Jesse and Hadassah live just down the street from our own cluster of houses. They have waited for years to be blessed with a child. Last night, she delivered a *tinoki*, but it was stillborn.

Hadassah is hysterical with grief. Some fear she is losing her mind.
Yosef urges me to spend as much time as possible with her since
her mother has gone to the Great Beyond, he
thinks I have a way of soothing her.
My own heart is so burdened.

28th Shevat

February 8th

DEAR DIARY,

Suzanna has practically planted her feet under our table.
It is not much of an inconvenience since Lydia and Ruthie are good
at keeping little Samuel occupied. He is starting to
play more with our youngest boys, also.

*Please, HaShem, hallowed be Thy Name, please, don't
let the Death Angel come here anymore!*

19th Adar

February 29th

DEAR DIARY,

Seeing you in my trunk today was like meeting a *chavivi* (friend) as I
read various portions from long ago, which brought back
happier memories.
It is not like old times, having Suzanna and Hadassah around so
much, but I think they are healing and soon will be going.
Suzanna is thinking about selling the farm with
the help and advice of some of the elders.
Yeshua is taking over the carpentry shop because
Yosef tires more as he grows older.
When I see him step into the house with his face looking
so white and strained, my heart tightens with fear. What can be the
matter? Yosef is too young to have health problems, but he did have a
sister who was snatched away by the Death Angel as a youthful virgin.

He wouldn't have wanted me to know, but a friend admitted
she had seen him step into the physicians' house on more than
one occasion—without even an adze hooked in his belt!
Yaakov, Jude and Jose are also learning the carpenter's trade,
but they will never achieve the quality of workmanship
Yeshua has acquired because their hearts are not in it.
I don't think anyone could, for that matter.
For Yeshua, it is an art; it is providing us a
respectable living in spite of all the taxes.
Someday, not too soon I hope,
Yeshua will lay down His tools and walk away from our lives. I sadly
remember He is meant for greater things than just carpentry.
I keep wanting to poke holes through the veil of time to see what the
future holds, but I suppose it is best if we do not know too much.

Marilyn Friesen

24th Sivan

June 2nd

DEAR DIARY,

Someone who had business at the shop today said Zadok
had been seen in the country of the Gergesenes.
He was obviously looking for
work. His raiment was worn and tattered.
What has happened to the dear, friendly boy that used to come
running into the shop with his father, all eager to see and do so
many different things?
Oh dear, I guess he is still the same boy, but he just got
carried away seeing and doing the wrong sort of things.
Oh, *El Shaddai*, may he realize there are many blessings
awaiting him if he would just come home.

21ˢᵗ Adar

March 3ʳᵈ

DEAR DIARY,

Yeshua leaned against the door and turned a hammer over and over in His hands. I continued with my turning and punching of the bread dough, but could sense that He was troubled.

"What will it take for Zadok to come to himself," He sighed. I waited for Him to continue, when He didn't I looked up just in time to see Him wipe away a tear with His sleeve. "Have you heard any news?" He nodded in the dim morning light. "One of the camel boys from the caravan passing through came to buy a part for his master. He had seen it with his own eyes; Zadok is feeding swine! I'm afraid he thought it was hilarious. Zadok must be feeling so humiliated—and desperate!

"Swine: they are so repulsive to us Jews," Yeshua continued, "and now h is reduced to caring for them. The camel boy claims Zadok was eying a cob of field corn as if he was about to chomp on it, husks and all. They must not be feeding him well if he's that famished."

"We can't believe everything we hear, "I murmured, giving the dough a final pat, covering it with a linen towel.

He nodded. "But that isn't all I came to talk about. Abba is looking weak and exhausted already, we haven't even had our morning meal. He tries to work as hard as always, even though I suspect there is something wrong with his heart." I nodded and looked down at the dough cradled between my two hands. Yeshua stepped into the house and laid his hand on my shoulder. "Try to convince him to stay in for a little while after we break our fast. He thinks he must match his pace

with mine, even though I am now as strong he," His
voice dropped, "or perhaps much stronger."

"I'll try," my voice quavered.

"I must rush back. As usual, we are very busy."

Of course they are busy. Nowhere else could such excellent
workmanship be found other than in our
shop, yet our prices are reasonable.

I watched my tall son turn and stride out the door.
Where have the years flown? It seems like such a
little while ago I cradled Him in my arms and was
attending to His every need. Now He is a man.

29th Adar

March 11th

DEAR OLD DIARY,

I will turn to you in my hour of greatest need. For some time, my *Chavivi* has been ill and I have been so uneasy. Some things are just too dreadful to cope with. I put off the inevitable for too long, but I must not avoid writing about this day no matter how much it hurts.

"Yosef, are you feeling alright?" I asked, hovering over him as
he took a long draught of water in the middle of the night.
It seems like worry shadows my every step these days.

"I am sorry I woke you, *Chavivi*. Why don't you try to
get back to sleep?" *He didn't answer my question.*
"You will come to bed, yes?"
Yosef shrugged his shoulders, in the dim moonlight that
filtered through the window his face looked haggard, drawn.
"I think I will go sit on the rooftop for a while."
"But it's raining out!"
"Just a fine drizzle . . . I will be alright."
"Mind if I go with you?"
He hesitated, then shook his head. "You need your
sleep, *Chavivi*. I will be along after a bit."
I wrapped my arms around him, crushing myself against his chest.
He kissed my hair, then gently lifted my face to look into my eyes.
"Try not to worry, sweetheart. Everything will be alright."
My throat constricted. Everything was not alright. I knew it, and he
knew it, but he had not said things were all right, but that they would
be. It was hard to hang on to such a thin strand of hope.
"Please, let me go with you!" I pleaded.
He sighed, "I will come back to bed.
We wrapped our arms around each other as if we would never
let go. I used to love going to sleep with my head on his chest,

but not anymore. The way his heart was beating didn't always sound right; it made me ill at ease. He has admitted to me that sometimes he has severe pain in his chest. We have discussed it in the past, but I did not want to even mention it tonight, because I knew I couldn't control my emotions.. Yosef knew how I was feeling, and brushed at my tears with the edge of the blanket.

"Oh, Yosef!"

"Mary'am, as long as I live, I will take care of you and cherish you. As long as you live, remember how precious you are to me. I hope that will be a comfort."

I tried to hold back a sob but he heard it anyway, and gently stroked my hair. I snuggled in closer and we clung together as if our clinging could keep the Death Angel from snatching him away.

Sometime after I had fallen asleep, Yosef slipped away and climbed up the ladder to the rooftop. A cooling breeze was blowing, a fine mist hovered over everything. As soon as I awoke, I climbed up the ladder, filled with anxiety, dreading the worst.

Yosef was kneeling beside the balustrade with his hands clasped as if in prayer, yet pressed forcefully against his rib cage. His *tefilah* shawl was draped around his shoulders. The mist had enriched its colors, making the white glisten like snow, the blue as lovely as the sea, sky and Heaven it was meant to represent. For some reason, it reminded me of the tabernacle tent in the wilderness. Shekinah dwelt there, and there beneath Yosef's prayer shawl, deep in his heart, was *El' Shaddai's* presence.

He turned and smiled faintly at me, but I saw that his face was ashen, caused by extreme pain. He sagged towards me and I rushed forward, sensing he had waited for me to come. I lay his head on my bosom. It was my turn to caress his hair now. I heard him speak indistinctly and bent closer to catch what he was trying to say.

"Hear, oh Yisrael, the Lord our *El Elohim*, the Lord is
One," he sighed faintly as the spirit left his body.

"Extolled, hallowed be the name of *El Elohim* throughout the world
which He has created," I murmured brokenly. . . . Just is He in
all His ways. Praise be the Lord of Life, the righteous Judge."

The sun broke over the horizon, lighting the clouds with a silvery
radiance. I sat there with his head on my lap for an hour or so,
till Yeshua came looking for us.
He knelt and put His arm around me,
we gazed together at the dear face of the one
we both cared about so deeply.

"He was a good Abba to me," Yeshua's voice broke.

I nodded, tears coursed down my cheeks. Yosef
had been a good Abba. He was so
brave to accept me as an unwed mother
and share the scorn of a critical world when he didn't have to take on
such a responsibility. I recalled the times he had been hotly accused
of snatching the grapes before they were ripe 'by some of my
male relatives, but he had never protested vehemently.
Once he had murmured, "things are not always as they
appear," but when pressed for an explanation,
he just walked away.
There could be such a stillness about him at such times that
even the clamorous, most excitable hecklers gave up.
The rest of the household was waking up,
I heard one child then another calling "Imma!" Soon
enough, they all found their way to the rooftop.

Lydia was holding Ruthie's hand, Yaakov and
Jose were jostling each other to see who could get up the ladder first.
Their laughing voices fell silent when they saw the scene of sorrow.

I motioned for them to come closer,
Ruthie buried her head on my shoulder while Lydia
squeezed in as close as she could. Yeshua put his arms around
his younger brothers and lifted the youngest one on His lap.
We just sat there staring at Yosef.

"Let not your hearts be troubled," Yeshua said gently. "We
believe in *El Elohim*. He will prepare a home in Paradise for each
one of us." We nodded sadly and just snuggled in closer...

Soon enough, the word would spread that my highly respected
carpenter husband had gone to the Great Beyond,
friends would be seeking to bring us comfort. I will appreciate
each one of them, but at that moment I just wanted to
hold my family close, to cherish them with all my
heart. I want this scene to be imprinted on my mind forever.
Now, my beloved family circle is broken. But as long as we could see
my husband and the children's father, it does not seem so final.
Soon, they will come and take his body away, but
for this moment we could still cling together.

19th Adar

March 1st

DEAR DIARY

What an empty, empty bed. I can hardly bear to crawl beneath my covers night after night. It feels so cold and I do not know what exactly, but I dread the night!

Sometimes, the haunting awareness that Yosef is gone briefly escapes me during the day when I must need be going about my work and caring for our children, but the loneliness is almost impossible to bear after everyone is sleeping.

Last night, my daughters brought their pallets closer because I know they are suffering also.
At first, I wanted to be brave and I tried not to cry in their presence but Lydia sensed that something was wrong. She bent over, laid her cheek against my cheek and suddenly all of us were hugging each other while the tears pooled in our eyes.

While sharing memories, we even laughed a little. It was good for all of us. Maybe that is the better way, instead of trying to pretend I am so strong when I'm not. Yeshua was doing the same for the boys in the other chamber.

I know our little crying session drew us closer together. It is a rather tight squeeze in our tiny space but we slept surprisingly well. I think it was because we all needed the security of someone we could snuggle up to even in our slumbers. Our people aren't prone to hiding their emotions, we are able to share them freely.

It will be hard raising such a handful of rambunctious boys and their sisters without Yosef's steady guiding influence.

DEAR DIARY,

I wearily admit it is high time that Lydia is wed, but I can't
bear to let her go just now. She has been such a help to me.
I hope Michael bar Joseph can be patient.
I trust so, he is so calm and steady compared to our impulsive
talkative Lydia. Before Yosef passed, his parents and
we agreed they would make a good match.

How manly Yeshua has become!
I am sure He has been thinking of starting out on His own in whatever
way *Adonai* wishes Him to since He is already past twenty, but for
my sake, He has laid all plans aside. He will support the family
until the younger boys are mature enough to take over. He has not
actually said so, but His attitude portrays as much since Yosef died.

*Oh Yeshua, Yeshua, what would I do without you? You are such a
comfort to me and yet so many homes--nay, all homes . . . have to
muddle along without someone like You to lean on! The pain of losing
my dear husband is easier to bear because You abide with us.*

DEAR DIARY,

I have not written in here very much lately. My thoughts have been
filled with Yosef and I know I will ruin this expensive parchment
if it is dampened, so today I will be extra careful not to weep.

The empty ache of loneliness just goes on and on. The girls
seem to cry more easily and the boys get into scrapes often.
I heard a comment lately that really tore at my heart.
"Well, Mary'am, if you would have just humbly admitted
that he wasn't the father of your firstborn, perhaps *HaShem*
wouldn't have taken him taken from your side."
"Yeshua?" My hand flew to my breast. *Surely not…*
"No, foolish woman, your husband."
I stammered incoherently as she babbled on,
but comprehended not another word.
The children heard it all. Yaakov, yea and Simeon also, would have run
after her shouting if I hadn't restrained them.(Not that I wanted to.)

DEAR DIARY,

There was a beam of light shining through the clouds today, both literally and in my spirit. I was able to slip out of my mantle of grief for a spell.

A wonderful thing happened.
Plump, wealthy Martha, the mother of our dear
friend, Zadok, came bustling down our street.
She seemed to be calling a greeting at every door.
We were all surprised to see her in person, and on foot, but I guess
she was too eager to tell us the news, rather than rely on a servant.

Zadok has returned. *Amen, Alleluia Elohim!*
And at Rosh Hashanah at that! It seems like the whole
neighbourhood has been invited to their
place for a feast next week to help celebrate.
Yosef would have so happily attended, but nay, I
will not pine for that which cannot be.

DEAR DIARY,

What a gala occasion! You wouldn't have recognized Zadok from
the rumors we heard about him. He was freshly bathed, his hair was
trimmed and his father had him clad
in the most wonderful raiment of pure silk, sewn in stripes of
purple and saffron. That purple wasn't tinted with the common
vegetable dye that most people use either. It was stained with
the liquid from the murex shell, which is far more expensive.
In outward appearance, he was somewhat the same, taller,
leaner perhaps, but at the same time different.
He looked humble, almost sheepish, perhaps due to all the
attention, yet there was a quiet happiness about him as well.
Oh, if only all of *El Shaddai*'s wandering sheep could realize how gladly
their Heavenly Father would welcome them back; my heart aches
for other mothers in Yisrael who are weeping over their prodigals.
I made myself comfortable on one of the many mats scattered
throughout the festive rooms and placed a cushion
behind my back up against the wall.

Zadok was reclining on a couch beside the table with the men.
Eventually, he excused himself and sat beside me. I know it is considered
improper for a man to converse with a woman, but he has felt just like
one of my boy for so many years. I hoped no rebbes present would
frown too darkly upon us, thus spoiling the joyous occasion.

"It is so good to see you back, Zadok."

"That's what everyone says," he grinned self-consciously. "I
feel so unworthy of all that my father has done for me.
Why, my parents treat me like a prince!
I feel so *niphal*, for how I disgraced Abba's honorable name,

Marilyn Friesen

but he thinks nothing of it.

"Mary'am, when I came plodding down the road, I stank like
swine! Loathsome swine, can you envision that? I was filthy.
But Abba was looking for me."
his voice broke and he looked down for a moment
before continuing.
"Every day, at least once or twice, he walked a little way down
the road and shaded his eyes to see if I was coming.
He could have dragged me home long ago, whipped me like
a common slave, but no, he wanted me to choose for myself
whether I would return to my Father's house, or nay."

Zadok buried his head in his hands. "To think I left all this—"
he motioned with his hand, "for a life of iniquity."
A servant stood by with an amber glass pitcher filled with fragrant
pomegranate juice and waited for a lull in the conversation.
"Care for some more to drink?"

A sweet, talitha, gaily decked in a saffron yellow wimple, followed
with a platter. An artistically arranged combination of dates from the
Jordan Valley and locally harvested almonds were arrayed upon it.

"Care for something good to eat?" she chirped." These
dates are the freshest, the best-tasting in the country!"

We each took a little of what was offered,
Zadok continued with his story. "Oh, of course I thought I was
having a great deal of fun, but each pleasure enticed me
to go deeper into sin. I was never satisfied.
Eventually, it dawned upon me that I was paying for all of the lavish
parties, my money was running short. I wasn't worried. I figured my
new-found comrades would pitch in and help if I asked them to.
"It didn't work that way. It really was hard on me when I had to sell my
stallion, but I knew he was worth a lot of money and I didn't want
him to get run down because of inadequate feed."

He took a small sip. "I wasted so many months in riotous living." He gazed thoughtfully across the room, focusing on nothing in particular. "If I learned anything from the experience, I would say that there is nothing more important than a good relationship with family, and being accepted by *HaShem*."

I felt uneasy. *How can anyone truly feel accepted by HaShem?* I knew Yeshua did, but that was different, and now Zadok seemed assured of *El Elohim*'s approval.

I swirled my drink, watching the tiny wave that formed, as we sat in companionable silence.

Soon, Zadok was called away, someone else came to sit down beside me, but I found it hard to initiate a conversation. All my life I have tried so hard to be good, but I don't feel as free in *El' Elohim's Shekinah* as Zadok does. Will it ever change? Is it a blessing reserved for the privileged few until, until what?

Later, I noticed that Zadok's brother, Malachi, was missing. I went to the door to look for him. Out in the starlight, his father was heading towards him with his arms outstretched. Malachi was shaking his head about something.

As they drew nearer, Hezekiah sounded amazed. "But all that I have is available to you!"

Even though I merged in with the shadows, so as not to disturb their private moment, I noticed that Malachi had turned away, he did not follow his father back into the mansion.

2nd Nissan

March 13th

DEAR DIARY,

Yeshua is so good to me.

It had been a hard day, rainy and misty just like
the day Yosef my *Chavivi* passed away.

I was looking forlornly out the window when I heard a voice
behind me. It took me a moment to realize it was Yeshua's; it
sounded so manly, yet kindly and mellifluous.

"Come unto me."

I looked up wondering, He lifted His hands beseechingly to me.

"Come unto me. You are laboring and heavy-laden,
I want to help you find rest for your spirit."

"You, Yeshua?" I laid my hands on his shoulders while searching His
eyes. There is something about His serene spirit that alleviates my
care.

"Yea, Me. I know that My hour has not yet come, but when it does, I
long to give rest . . . rest to you, to all of this weary troubled world."

He smiled down at me. "You believe, Imma, that I am He; that's
why I venture to say what I do. I will give you what reassurance
I can, even now, but when I am imbued with power, I will give
you even more of that blessed comfort that comes from above."

"You are such a joy already, my son."

DEAR DIARY,

I do not see Yeshua very often anymore and it makes me desperately lonely. He lovingly helped care for us until He was thirty-years-old, and then Jose took over the carpenter shop. His brethren, all married now, have set up their own businesses.

Rachael, the little friend Yeshua used to play with long ago, married her childhood playmate, Asher, and now Rachael's lovely daughter is about to be wed.

Yeshua has gathered a small group of followers and goes about teaching, but I do hope He will be able to attend this wedding, Especially since it is His old friends, Asher and Rachael, whose talitha is to be wed.

21ˢᵗ Tishri

October 19ᵗʰ

DEAR DIARY,

As we plodded along over hill and dale,
the faint line of olive and cypress
trees in the distance told us that we were nearing our
destination. We arrived at *Khirbet Qana* (Cana) mid-
afternoon on the day before the wedding festivities began.

As usual, I found it delightful to watch the ten virgins arrive with
their lamps, to be brightly lit later in the evening.
It was good to see that they all had their vials of extra oil
dangling from their fingers. It makes me feel sad when one of
the virgins is turned away because her lamp has gone out.
Their job is to herald the coming of the bridegroom.
Every one of them looked so sweet and pure, so
radiantly happy in their snowy white garments.

Snow never lasts long in our area, but when it comes,
it soon looks dingy. I've been to Mt Hermon, however,
which has plenty of snow, it is dazzling!

At one wedding, not too long ago, some of the virgins had fallen
asleep before the governor had called upon them to search
'for the bridegroom, their lamps had gone out. I am so
glad that didn't happen at Michal's wedding!

Any weariness I may have been feeling, from being
up so late, faded like mist when I first saw those ten
human *angels*, and later Yeshua, in the crowd.

"Yeshua, it is good to see you once again!" I said, touching Him on the
sleeve. While He pressed my head against his shoulder, my tears of

happiness brimmed over. The brightly-colored throng pressing
around nearly separated us, but I just clung to Him harder.
Gently, He moved me back, placing His strong hands
on my shoulders. He looked into my eyes and said,
"You are looking well, Imma, but how are you
feeling?"

I knew he was aware of my deep loneliness, caused by losing
the love of my life. "I miss him, still," I swallowed, "but time
does have away of taking away the sharp edge . . . I guess."

"You will join us, yes? José or Jude can take care of your little house . . .
rent it out perhaps, and you can be in our company for a while."

"Do you think that would work? I would love to. I am sure you do not
take time to eat properly, but if I could make the meals . . ." He silenced
my flow of words with a finger on my lips, saying it surely would work.

Someone interrupted us to speak to Yeshua. It thrilled my heart to
hear him being given the respected title of Rebbe. In later years,
He would even be called Rabboni, the most respected title of all.

I turned to greet an elderly uncle, whom I had not seen for quite
some time. Yeshua and I were separated by the joyous multitude.
It was so good to be at a wedding once again.
Weddings are such a wonderful opportunity to catch up on
news with loved ones. Salome was very happy because it was her
only granddaughter that was to be wed. I could not help but
remember that long ago day when Rachael and Yeshua had
excitedly raced out with hands clasped to help with the seeding.
Now Rachael was the mother of three fine sons and
one daughter, Michal, who had found someone to go hand in
hand with for the rest of her life. How the time has flown.

I wonder if Yeshua will ever have the opportunity to
be married. Why has not He chosen a bride?

Or more significantly, supported any of the choices
we had made for Him? More than a dozen *talitha*
would have gladly been betrothed to Him.

Salome and I found a little time to talk so we secluded
ourselves on a quiet bench on the veranda.
The abundant grape vines, with their
luscious drooping fruit, offered a pleasant shelter from the sun's rays.
Salome asked one of the passing servants to bring us each a glass of new
wine. He paused, bowed slightly, hesitated and then said,
"I will see what I can do."

As he started to leave, Salome called out to him, "Is there a problem?"
"I am sorry, but we are running out of wine. There are several
days of feasting left, but because of the heat and unusually large
number of guests, there will not be enough.to go around."

Salome and I gazed at each other in consternation. What could
be more distressing than running out of wine at a wedding
feast? Some would consider it a bad omen, even. By the looks
of things, an unusually large number of guests had shown up,
probably because they had heard that Yeshua would be there.

Yeshua was walking nearby, flanked as usual
by His talmidim, (disciples).

"Yeshua," I called softly to get His attention. He
turned and looked expectantly at me.

"They have no wine," I said, knowing full well that He could
somehow help just as He had often come to my aid in the past.
I have a memory of him struggling with a foaming pail of goat's
milk that He was trying to carry in for me, just one of many
pleasant memories. His smock was sopping, I remember.

Yeshua smiled indulgently at me, and when He spoke,
I heard that teasing lilt that I love so much.

"Madam, what have I to do with you? My hour is not yet come."

We exchanged a warm smile, I knew He would want to do
something about the problem just like he had many times before.

I turned to the servants and said, "Do whatever He asks of you." I
had no idea what He might do, but I had confidence, knowing that
He wouldn't leave Raddai and Michal in an awkward situation.

There were six water pots made of stone, each containing two or three
firkins a-piece, in our vicinity. I watched with interest as Yeshua
told the servants to fill them to the brim with water, which they
did, casting amused looks at each other. But when He told them
to bring the governor of the feast the first drink, they protested.

"This is only water," one exclaimed. "The Master will think that we are
fools, or that we are making fun of him for running out of wine; either
way, we will be disgraced and we may even lose our jobs!"

"Just do it," He answered firmly. Even though the servants may not
have known who Yeshua was, since He had not been to this quiet
hill town for many years, there was an authority
about Him that caused them to obey.

I would have loved to have trailed after them to see the
governor's response, but that is not the ladylike thing to
do, especially for an *aant'at* of my age. I just sat there in
the cool shade chatting pleasantly with Salome.
Fortunately we weren't long in finding out what had happened.
Salome's young grandson came rushing up to us.

"Mimi, Mimi" (Grandma), he cried, "you should have seen
what just happened. It was a miracle. I am sure of it.

This wonderful Rabboni was there,
He told the servants to fill the water pots with water. Me an' some
of my friends watched them do it because we knew that the
wine was gone. We tagged along to see what the master of
ceremonies would do when he tasted the water. He was amazed.
He said he had never tasted such delec—delec-
delectable wine in all his life!"
His friend interrupted, "I got to taste it, it was very good.
It did not make me sick or woozy or nothing, either!"
Salome smiled at the excited children. "What
did the governor of the feast say?"

"He called over to the bridegroom"—Sadoc reported, "Dohd Raddai,
I mean, and, well, I can't remember the exact words but it was
something like, 'Why did you leave the good wine 'til the last?'"

"Of course, Michal wanted to taste it also," Eshban added
enthusiastically, "as did Asher and Rachael, Yahdeil, and oh,
just everybody. Soon, everyone was asking to have their cups
refilled and they wanted to know where it had come from."

"One of the servants told everyone that it came straight from the
well," Sadoc continued," and at first they didn't believe it.
When other hired men constantly reaffirmed that it was
so, everyone was so thrilled. It was a man named Yeshua
who was 'sponsible for turning the water into wine."

He stopped and looked at me closely, "Are you not his imma?"

I nodded. Just then, someone came with a pitcher and filled our
wine glasses; the boys raced off. As we sipped the most delectable
wine I had ever tasted, Salome and I glanced knowingly at
each other. She also knew there was something
special about my first born.

Surely His hour has come, we thought as we rose simultaneously
to mingle once more with the wedding guests.

It was a long time before Salome and I had time to ourselves again,
but when we did, we asked each other if we should both go to be
Yeshua's helpers on His many missionary journeys.
Now that Salome is also a widow,
it felt like something worthwhile and certainly something rewarding
that we could do for the young man that we both loved so well.

11th Cheshvan

October 27th

DEAR DIARY,

Neither Salome or I were able to go right away, but when Yeshua left on the morning of the fourth day, I hurried home to get my house in order so I could attend Him later.

Michal wished that the celebrations could have lasted much longer, like they do among the wealthy, but she knew we poor villagers could not afford such extravagance.

21ˢᵗ Adar

March 3ʳᵈ

DEAR DIARY,

Finally I can go!

I enjoyed travelling through the fresh sunlit countryside, but it wasn't long before we were buffeted by heavy winds. I clung tightly to my shawl to keep it from blowing away, to prevent the billowing dust from stinging in my eyes. I soon realized it would be difficult to keep up with the steady gait of Yeshua and His talmidim; they scarcely slackened their pace because of the gale but were determined not to complain.

What if He decided it was too hard for me and then took me back? Exhausted though I was,
I delighted in trudging along a few steps behind, even if
I was only hearing snatches of their conversations.
I sensed that the *a'Ahava*, deep love, that has always emanated
from His *Shekinah* was growing stronger with every passing
year. It was enough for me to be in sight of Him,
whom I loved dearly, although I feel so unworthy to be useful to Him.
His talmidim are keeping Him busy with their many
comments and queries as we journey from place to place.
It was such a blessing to hear Him discuss a sermon He
had preached near the hamlet of *Tabgha*. It sounded
like such wonderful constructive advice.

At first, His every sentence had begun with the word *'banoah'*, which surely indicates that *Adonai* wants His followers to be happy.
What a blessed kingdom He is preparing to rule!
Never before have I realized how important it is to keep our thoughts pure, meek and so on because what we think is able to have a surprizing amount of influence on those around us.

Shortly after that, Yeshua fell in step with me. "How are you making out, Mother?" He asked gently.

"A little tired," I confessed, "but I will be fine."
"Shall we rest?"
"Nay, I will be fine."

"Here, have some." He handed me a flask of water.
"Maybe you are thirsty."
I half expected it to be new wine but it was refreshing clear cool water. "Do not worry about me, *tinoki,*" I said, softly enough for only His ears to hear. "It is enough just to be in your Shekinah." He nodded gravely, my heart nearly melted from the warmth in His eyes. That night, we stopped, I suspect earlier than they normally would Have, because I was not yet used to being on the road for so long.

They visited around a small fire long after I was supposedly asleep. It disturbed me that those rough country men could be so loud and opinionated in the presence of the Son of *El Elohim*. *Know they not who their Teacher is?* Yet, His soothing wise answers soon lulled me to sleep.

There must have been a slight change in the tenor of their voices, the wind, or something else caused me to waken an hour or so later. Yeshua was sharing His experiences in the wilderness. My heart filled with pity when He mentioned not eating for forty days. He had not eaten at night either. Those must have been lonely terrifying nights.

Did the hyenas howl close by; did those ugly vultures swoop, eager to get at His carcass whenever He lay down? Or did He even lie down? Did the dear Son of *El Elohim* just pace back and forth, so deep in communion with His Heavenly Father that when weariness and hunger gripped Him He just transferred the anguish into stronger entreaties to His Father *El Elohim*? *Would that I could do that better.*

What did He pray for? Who did He pray for? What were the cries of His loving heart? Bone of my bone, flesh of my flesh, but we are worlds apart when it comes to true spiritual understanding.

I have heard somewhat about Lucifer, the fallen angel, but
I had not realized how much trouble he can cause
until I listened to Yeshua describe what happened after
He had gone without food for nearly six weeks.

Lucifer recommended that Yeshua turn some stones into bread. I can picture which stones they were. Some very much resemble little loaves of flatbread and He could have easily thought, *all I would have to do is to eat one, no one need ever know that I did. I am so very famished, strength is desperately needed in order to make that wearisome journey back to civilization.* He could have even tried to convince Himself that maybe it was *El'Elohim* who had brought the idea to His mind.

I do not know how long He hesitated, but I do know what His response was, '*It is written, Man shall not live by bread alone but by every word that proceedeth out of the mouth of El Elohim.*'

Oh, I am so thankful that Yeshua carefully worked at His lessons while He was in school and still knows so much of the Scriptures by heart!

23rd Shevat

February 3rd

DEAR DIARY,

The next night, Yeshua described two other temptations that the devil had tried to entice him with. I got a clearer picture of just how awful it must have been. I'll try to describe it here.

After many hours of pacing in the heat of the day, Yeshua weakly sank down and leaned against one of the sunbaked boulders.

He observed the smooth oval rocks in front of him. *Maybe these are actually loaves of bread,* he dizzily thought. *My heavenly Father knows how desperately hungry I am.* He started to reach out to them then drew His hand back. *Nay, I told Satan that I would not turn these stones into bread, even if I just touched them, I know there is enough power in My body to transform them into food. In my famished state, I couldn't help but devour them. But that would make Satan the winner.*

His mouth began to water at the prospect of crunching on fresh, tasty loaves, so He got up to get His mind away from His desperate need for nourishment. The heat, the fatigue and the hunger were draining Him. This had been causing Him to feel very weak and haggard for many days already.

"Cast Thyself down . . . cast Thyself down . . ." A voice, sweeter, yea smoother than melted honey, breathed into His ear.

I am cast down. I've never been at a lower point in My life. Is it really true that My Heavenly Father spoke to Me, and the Spirit descended in the form of a dove? Do I really have a purpose in life? Nay, no, I must not doubt it! He called Me His Chavivi Son. Right now, I feel so very weak, it's hard to grasp that this is who I truly am.

Yeshua forced Himself to start walking around in an effort
to try to eliminate the continually oppressive thoughts. *Why
are you so cast down, oh my soul, and why are you disquieted
within me? If I really am the son of El Elohim, why am I so
despondent?*

I did not quite understand if Yeshua had been led to the pinnacle of
the temple or if 'twas in a vision that He went there, but I did not want
to interrupt His story to ask Him. Once
again, that sickeningly sweet voice
spoke into His ear. *"If you are the son of El Elohim,
show your power by casting yourself down."*

Yeshua sorrowfully realized that showing His power in such
a dramatic fashion would not change the hearts of men.
Men were born with the seed of sin, many of them wanted
to do that which was evil. He would not force them to do
good. He loved them too much not to give them
the power to choose what they wanted out of life.

In some ways, this must have been the hardest temptation of
all, because He wanted so much to make them happy,
but it had to be their own choice.
Besides, if they weren't cleansed from sin by sacrificial blood,
there could be no permanent victory or redemption for them.

Another thought must have weighed on His heart.
If He worshiped Satan, who was so evil, He would be
evil also and could never show compassion to the human
race even if He had wanted to at one time.
He turned on His adversary and rebuked him sharply.
"Get thee hence, Satan. For it is written,
*Thou shalt worship the Lord thy
El Elohim, and him only shalt thou serve!*"

To my great relief, and I am sure Yeshua's also,
Satan left him for a season, although
I do wish I knew how long that was. Oh, I am so glad that His
heavenly Father sent angels to minister to him at that time.
It must have been such a wonderful blessing to have
visitors from His heavenly home after enduring such
severe afflictions, both physical and spiritual.

25th Av

August 1st

DEAR DIARY,

Another thought just occurred to me, after those sweet angels soared
down to care for my ailing son, He must have felt like a renewed
man. He had just gone through the severest trial anyone has
ever been asked to suffer, and had come forth victorious.
Selah, (Pause and calmly think about what I have just said.)

I'd like to have seen them.
I wonder what those cheerful angels said or did for Him?
His heavenly home must have seemed delightfully near and
pleasant; they probably talked about His heavenly Father.
Without a doubt, Yahweh was well pleased with how
courageously Yeshua withstood temptation in the wilderness.
I guess no one will really know what they communed
about, but Yeshua came forth imbued
with power and with a deep assurance that He
must be about His Father's business.
I remember Him coming home shortly after this, thin,
worn and gaunt-looking, but He hadn't stayed long and was
in no mood to discuss what He had gone through.

DEAR DIARY,

We moved to K'far Nahum, Capernaum, after Yosef died and I was glad to be away from Navara. It was with mixed emotions, therefore, that I saw that His face was set to go to our former hometown. I wondered how He would be received there.

I went along with Him and also to the synagogue, although women frequently stay home. I was somewhat surprised that the ruler handed him a scroll which indicated that He was being invited to read from the Torah and speak about it.

My attention was distracted by whispering voices just behind me.

"Well, look at that. They are actually expecting Yeshua-bar—Yosef to speak!"

"Humph, it was never proven that he was Yosef's son. I don't see any likeness in him."

"Neither do I. I can't place him. He looks like he could be any man's son. Fancy them letting him speak!"

"Well, they mustn't consider him a bastard then. Otherwise, they would keep him from entering the building, no?"

"Hush! My, what gracious words are coming out of his mouth… I am sure that is not the reading for today."

My ears had grown hot while this dialogue was taking place but for a moment the gossipers became quiet.

"What? What nerve! He's taking the words of Isaias and twisting them to apply to himself. Look how flustered is the reader. Obviously, it wasn't today's reading."

"SHH!"

"This is infuriating! I hope someone stops him!"

"Look! Your husband has jumped up and is trying to reason with him!"

"Reasoning?" a new voice muttered. "It looks more like berating to me. Another man has joined him, and another. Are we going to have an uprising right here in the house of *HaShem*?"

By then, nearly everyone in the women's balcony was rising from their seats, craning their necks to get a better view.

I marveled at how unperturbed He was even after the men started pulling and shoving at Him. As the shouting increased, I had also risen from my seat; with my hand to my throat, I watched as they grew angrier, more violent. The names of the Holy One were on my lips.

"Yeshua!" I wailed as they dragged Him out of the building.

When I heard someone yell, "Throw him over the brow of the hill," I struggled to reach the exit. It was impossible! Everyone was fighting to get out. A wee talitha screamed, she was being crushed by the press of bodies. I picked her up and held her high above my head. Her mother snatched her from me and continued pushing her way towards the stairs.

I hung back. There was no getting through the congestion, too many people. I went to look over the balustrade. The synagogue had almost completely emptied. A stooped old man was picking himself up off the floor, groping for his cane, tottering towards the open doors.

Marilyn Friesen

I could hear the shouting, the yelling from my position on the balcony. I collapsed, lifting my hands imploringly up to *Elohim*.

"*HaShem*, hallowed be Thy name, have mercy! Have mercy on Thy Son, oh Most High!" I whispered.

An ominous silence filled the building. Everyone else was gone. I continued praying, entreating *El Elohim* until no more words came, then I laid my head on the railing, my heart pounded. I lifted my head. The sounds were getting louder. They were coming back! *Where is Yeshua*, I wondered? I was staring through the wide open doors, looking at the multitude tramping down the road when a hand touched my shoulder. I looked up. "Yeshua! You escaped!" I started to fling myself at Him but He drew back. "They are searching for me. We must go quickly. We will slip out the back door." We snatched up our belonging, which were stowed nearby, and hurried, walking several furloughs out of town before stopping to rest. The disciples eventually caught up with us.

And now as I sit beneath a sycamore tree, writing it all down, I still feel shaky, but we are safe for now. I wonder why His *talmidim* did not try harder to protect Him, but at least He is safe.

I understand now, He merely walked through the midst of the mob without them even noticing. How can that be? *It sounds like a miracle to me!* My heart beat erratically for a long time afterward. *Please, El Shaddai, there is nothing more important to me than to see my children safe and happy.*

2nd Cheshvan

October 18th

DEAR DIARY,

I traveled with Him through the long hot summer. Some other women, including Salome, joined us. He didn't do quite as much traveling over the next winter, and when He did I couldn't come along except on bright sunny days, lest I become ill.

27th Tevet

January 9th

DEAR DIARY,

It is good to be back on the road with Him again. I wonder how many
more years I'll be able to care for Him on His missionary journeys
before I am too old and feeble?

We are at least twenty-five, maybe thirty furlongs, (just a
few miles) away from the town of my birth. The morning
sun is peeking over the eastern hills, crowning the deep
blue waters of the Sea of Galilee with all its glory.

I am sitting off to one side, observing what is going on around
me. Already the crowds have swelled into the hundreds. When I see
them all seeking, longing…needing… to be close to Yeshua,
it seems like my heart is in my throat much of the time.

Every so often, a beggar, a cripple, or some
other person who is usually looked
down upon, considered the lowest of the low, makes his or her way
to Yeshua's feet. There, they find comfort and healing.

The *talmidim* have tried to form a barrier around Yeshua to
protect Him from the jostling crowd but it really is quite useless.
That will be all for now. He seems to be done with today's
healing and is about to speak.

His words are more to be desired than gold, yea, even finely
wrought gold jewellery, sweeter than honey on the honeycomb.

Since I hunger to hear His divine messages, like all the rest, sometimes
I forget that I was the vessel that brought Him into the world. Yeshua
is called my son but He seems so much wiser, and more gracious than
I could ever be. With all my heart, I want to be more like Him.

DEAR DIARY,

About mid-morning, while we were strolling along
through the sunlit countryside, I saw one youngster snatch
a fold of His *tefilah* shawl in his hand, he shouted,

"I touched him, now I am a healer, too!" How Yeshua tolerated such
nonsense can only be attributed to what a kind-hearted man He is.
I am sure He is aware of every movement
around Him even while teaching.

This was the same day that He suddenly stopped in His tracks.
Several of the pushier sorts had walked on well ahead of
Him before realizing He was no longer walking as well.

"Who touched Me?" His voice rang out clearly.

I saw that same youngster shrink back behind someone's skirts,
but Yeshua's eyes were not searching him out.
The *talmidim* were bewildered that he would ask a question
like that surrounded by a mob, my curiosity
was aroused.

I caught sight of a stooped little old lady about the same time
Yeshua did. She had such a dazed but radiant look on her face, I
do not think she even noticed that the throng wasn't milling
around much anymore.
She wasn't even aware that some folks were staring at her,
while others were craning their necks to see why we had
stopped. When she saw that Yeshua wasn't too busy to give her heed,
she flung herself down at His feet, with tears of joy she babbled her
thanksgiving.

She had been suffering from some kind of bleeding disease, an ulcer
perhaps, and sensed that the moment she had touched His garment,
she was well again. Just think, to have been weakened from
loss of blood for such a long time, then to feel healthy in one
healing moment. How wonderful that must have been!
She was so happy, I think many of us basked in her joy,
although I did hear mutterings of discontent from a few.

"Daughter," He said, although I am sure she was older than
me by far, it didn't seem strange coming from Him,
"Your faith made you well; go in peace, be healed of your disease."

By the look on her face, I knew she was thinking, *all I did was
touch the fringe on His tefilah shawl!* I saw rapturous adoration in
her eyes just before the crowd once again closed around Him.

I humbly admit to adoring Him also. He seems like so
much more than my son. I did so little, if anything,
to mold Him into the gracious influential man that He is.
Not only is He respectful and considerate to men-folk, but
He is kind and gracious to even us poor lowly women.

That same day, a rebbe from the local synagogue spoke a few words
to Yeshua, requesting that He come and see his dying daughter.
My heart went out to Him when I saw the
anguish on His youthful intelligent face.
"Please, Rabboni, come quickly!" he begged,
"She may be dying at this very moment. We must get there!
It's urgent!"

Almost immediately, a messenger pressed through the crowd. "Jairus,
your daughter is dead." Then bitterly, "Why trouble ye the Master?"
Poor Jairus' spirit broke.
Our hearts poured out in sympathy for him.

To be so close to a healing for his child . . . to have it nearly within his grasp, then to have his hope snuffed out like a flickering flame. How heartbreaking! I think most of our petty vexations seemed to fall away before this sad loss; those closest to him offered words of consolation. I doubt if he even heard them.

His head was buried in his hands. It's awful to hear
the heart wrenching sobs of a fully-grown
man. It was their only child!

Yeshua touched the *rebbe's* shoulder and the synagogue leader looked up through tear-clouded eyes. "Fear not, only believe," Yeshua whispered.

I do not know what Jairus thought, but with head down, he led Yeshua over to his fancy house on the hill. I suppose it may well have been a tumble down shack as far as he was concerned, now that there was no echo of childish laughter to brighten his days.

It is getting dusky out and I will need to be up by sunrise to help make breakfast for Yeshua and His talmidim, so this will have to suffice for now.

DEAR DIARY,

Most of us were unable to squeeze into the house last night,
but we lingered outside, anxious to know
what would happen to the precious talitha.
We could hear the shrill wails of the hired mourners,
the sound of their pathos wrung my heart. I could picture the Imma
and Abba hovering over their lifeless *riba*, their faces careworn, while
glancing anxiously at Yeshua, wondering if He really could help them.

How I longed to have been inside,
to put my arms around that forlorn Imma's shoulders.
Everything went tomb-silent after the disgruntled mourners
filed out at Yeshua's request, I placed my finger
to my lips to hush a child's curiosity.
During the lull, I heard Yeshua's kind but commanding voice.
"*Talitha cumi!*", little girl, arise.
I think we collectively caught our breath when we heard a babble
of excited voices. Many inquisitive onlookers threw their manners
aside and stretched on tiptoe to peer in at the windows.
"She woke up!"
"Nay. Nay, she's alive!"
"Look at that! She's sitting up!"
"She's asking for water!"

The exclamations were relayed back to the rest of us as we
gazed at each other with tears of joy filling our eyes.
Suddenly, the door burst open, a girlish voice
exclaimed, "Why are all these people here?"
I wished I could have hugged her but I knew it would have
made her feel uncomfortable because I was a stranger.
Those that had crowded into the house poured out.

I noticed how the mother and father's faces absolutely glowed.

I went over to the *talithas'* mother, and clasped her
hand between mine. "I am so happy for you."

She hugged me like I was a long-lost friend,
then put her head on my shoulder and wept. I
cried with her. I saw Jairus clasp Yeshua's
hand and tell Him over and over how thankful he was.
By then, their daughter was dancing in their lovely courtyard with
several of her friends, they were singing at the top of their lungs.
Oh, how gracious *El Shaddai* is.
He was so merciful to bring their little daughter back from *Sheol*!

DEAR DIARY,

Poor Michal was frantic with worry today. Her young husband,
Raddai, went on a business trip with his father and would be back by
nightfall. For the first time in their short married life,
Michal was dreading his return. Somehow, she had lost
one of the dowry coins that had been fastened
to the hat below her wedding veil. Oh, she was so lovely and radiant
on her wedding day, but now her face was marred with tears.

"Mary'am!" Michal cried as she burst through the door,
"Mary'am, the most awful thing has happened!"
"What is it," I demanded, clutching her arm. "Is
it your Imma—or your Mimi Salome?"
"Nay, it is worse, far worse! Nay, nay, not worse but—
oh Mary'am, I have lost one of my dowry coins."
"Lost it! Oh, my darling *tinoki,* how could that be?"

We both knew this was no small loss. It wasn't only the value of the
coin, which was equivalent to a day's wages, but what it represented.
This was one of the dowry coins. If it was missing, the husband
could accuse his wife of using it to commit adultery,
and that was grounds for divorce.

Surely, *Raddai* would not be that hasty or hard-hearted, but I do
know that his father had not approved of his choice for a bride,
even though he gave his consent.
It was urgent that it be found.

Together we scurried over to their house, looking
high and low for that missing silver piece.
It was so dim inside, even with the door wide open.

In desperation, Michal lighted one of their few
precious candles as we continued searching.
I took it upon myself to sweep every corner of her
earthen floor and to shake out all the reed
mats and pallets while Michal busied herself with I know not what.
"Oh Michal, *Chavivi*," I mourned, "how did
you ever manage to misplace it?"
"I was caring for the neighbors' youngsters—such a rowdy lot they
are—when their parents went to that funeral in Cyros.

"It was after they returned to their home that
I noticed the coin was missing."
She carefully shook out her wedding garments, searching
among the folds, as she relayed the events.
I took another candle and lit it, examining all the cracks
at the edge of the room, lest it had rolled into one.

As the hours lengthened, our anxiety increased. Without a doubt,
the *drachma* would lose its color once it was ground into the dirt
and surely the inscription would be worn off.
How would it ever be found? We searched for hours.

"I found it!" Michal shrieked, holding it high in the air. Carefully,
we removed all the dirt, causing it to shine in its former glory.
Michal snatched it up once again and flew out the door.

"Rejoice with me!"
she called out to some *aant'at* strolling down the street.
They were on their way home from shopping and stared at her
in astonishment.

"Judith! Devora!—Hana—Naomi! Rejoice with me,
for I have found my lost coin!"

Eagerly, they rushed through the door admiring the
coin as if they had never seen a *drachma* before.

Naomi offered to fasten it back on to the hat while Rachael
opened a new cask of wine, diluting it with fresh well water.
Judith presented her freshly purchased basket of honey cakes
and dates for the feast, but before we could partake,
the younger ladies started dancing for joy. Of course those
small quarters could not contain such liveliness so the group
overflowed into the street. Other *Aleichem,* both young
and old, hurried over, eager to join in the merriment.

Although Naomi stayed behind, securing the coin to the wedding
hat, lest the cause for merriment disappear once again, I stood
in the doorway beaming at the carefree *aant'at.*

When I told the tale to Yeshua the next time I had an
opportunity, He got a thoughtful expression on his face.
It caused me to wonder if this incident would be
woven into one of His wonderful parables.

DEAR DIARY,

My younger sons have been aggravated for quite some time now. Yaakov and Shimon are the worst. They think Yeshua's teaching is too radical, and is affecting their reputation, their business. Personally, I think everyone's occupation is affected because of all the people surging after Him.
To tell you the truth, I am also worried,
although not for the same reasons.

The Pharisees are so opposed to Him. I find that hard to accept because they are religious leaders, supposedly sent from *El' Elohim*. Wouldn't it make more sense if they welcomed Him with gratitude? With all their learning, are they not able to comprehend that the *Mashiach* is come to fulfill the law and the prophesies It makes me nervous to think that their powerful body has held council against my so

9th Elul

August 27th

DEAR DIARY,

The Pharisees are saying that Yeshua is casting out devils through
Beelzebub, the prince of the devils. That is so outrageous!
Anyone can see that He is far too kind and good to do that.
Oh, I wish *HaShem* would stop their mouths.

When are they going to humble themselves and admit that Yeshua
was sent from above, that it is *El' Elohim* they are opposing?
In my heart, I've long suspected that our religious leaders are a
proud and haughty bunch, but it made me tremble to consider it.
If we can't trust them, whom can we trust?

19th Elul

September 6th

DEAR DIARY,

My adult sons have been pestering me to go with them to talk to
Yeshua. The crowds are numbering in the thousands already, and I
do not know how we will ever be able to get close to Him, but I have
agreed to try. They seem to think if I am with them, He would be more
inclined to listen to their complaints. They are determined to persuade
Him to temper His preaching. I don't have a *El Elohim* feeling about
taking this trip but I *am* concerned about His safety.

27th Elul

September 14th

DEAR DIARY,

It wasn't hard to find the house where He was staying.
It seemed like half the world was seeking after Him. Everyone we
met willingly gave us directions, but it was impossible to get inside
so we just looked in at the door.

The message was graciously relayed to Yeshua that we desired
to speak to Him. While we were waiting for His reply,
I watched the mingled responses to His sermon.
Many of the people leaned forward as if they were clinging to
His every word. When I saw how much they loved Him, how
many poor sufferers He had healed with just a loving touch,
I wondered, *What business have we to restrain Him?*

Yeshua had been stooping down to caress the hair of a little child
who had wrapped her arms around His legs when the messenger
spoke to Him. He straightened and looked directly at us.

"Who is my mother, or my brethren?"
His voice rang out so clearly
that my face flamed with embarrassment. There was a stirring, a
shrinking back among the people. They seemed shocked that He would
speak that way about His own family. I was stunned. *Why was He doing
this to us? Will He disown us without even knowing what we came for?*

I saw Yaakov and Shimon glare at each other, eyes flashing, even mild-
mannered Jose was angry, I wondered how my sons, the flesh of the love
between Josef and myself, could be so furious with their own brother?

Yeshua gazed affectionately, almost pityingly, at
those around Him and then met my eyes.

"Behold, my Mother and my brethren." In a heartbeat, it became clear to me. He had taken this opportunity to tell us as well as the others there, *"I have had a banoah relationship with my own family all these years, even though my brethren are angry with me just now. You also may be part of this rewarding relationship but on an even deeper, a spiritual level."* I admit, He was rebuking his brethren, and I suppose me also, for meddling in His affairs, but He also took this opportunity to tell us how close we can be to Him spiritually.

Oh, Yeshua, this rebuke hurt, but I am so glad for this opportunity to be Your mother. I'll try not to meddle ever again. Thank you, most Holy Father, for letting me have such a close relationship with Thy precious Son.

As we left for home, the yeled were still muttering among themselves, although I noticed how Jose and Jude slowly became more thoughtful. Someday, I trust they will believe in Him, but until then, I will just pray, be patient and rejoice that I am His and He is mine.

Marilyn Friesen

21st Tishri

September 19th

DEAR DIARY,

I have not been traveling with Yeshua and his *talmidim* much
lately because of all the rain. He did manage to spend this
Shabbat with me while His *talmidim* resided with friends and relatives.

Oh, what a quiet, peaceful, *banoah* it has been! It is often
so lonesome and quiet during the winter months because
both of my daughters have stayed in Navara. Suzanna and
Hadassah somehow managed to go on with their lives.

I was so happy when Yeshua took me aside and asked if I would take
a talitha into my home. I gladly agreed. Since her name is Mary'am,
the same as mine, I will call her by her Greek
name, Mary. She is a lovely maid, but has
suffered much. If all the talithas He finds are as sweet
as her, I would gladly open my home to them.

Yeshua was able to spare her from an awful death and I am so
glad. I suspect He has saved more than one daughter of Yisrael in
similar situations. I will paint a word picture of what happened.

MARY

The thin, wispy clouds were being tinted a peachy-pink by the setting sun. As Mary trudged slowly down the lonely city street, she was hardly aware that their glory reflected against the white of the buildings. She passed through the shadow of a large sycamore tree. Farther on, a playful breeze ruffled the leaves in a cluster of fig trees, tossing their coolness back to her. She did not notice at the time.

Three weeks ago, by that hour, Mary would have been busy grooming herself for her nightly occupation. Her profession had come to a halt when one of her more recent patrons had decided to make her a public example. Mary well remembered the first time he had stooped to enter her low door. It had taken a tremendous effort to conceal her shock since he was one of the leading Pharisees. Mary's parents had looked up to, nay, practically reverenced the words of this exact dark-black-bearded man.

Unfortunately, that was long ago. Her Abba and Imma had sunk to a watery grave when the ship they were taking to Phoenicia had capsized in a terrific gale while the moon shamefacedly hid its face behind a cloud. A thousand times, Mary had wished she had gone along on that journey.

But because she hadn't, she was forced to survive by the most ancient trade known to womankind, it was her only option. She had often pondered bitterly why no one showed *tzedakah*, mercy, compassion, justice, to her? If they didn't practice it, their Jewish lineage was supposed to be considered suspect, but it was as if her own

Jewishness was being held in question instead. Since no one seemed to remember the rule, many young girls ended up as *zonahs*, just like she had. What else could a helpless ignorant woman do?

Mary shivered as she recalled being dragged out of her bedchamber by that thin-nosed leader of the Jews. He had hauled her in front of a rebbe about whom she knew little, except that He seemed to do a lot of miracles. Mary had barely enough time to fling a blanket around her flimsy nightclothes before the crowd parted to let them through. How humiliating it had been, but it had taken scarcely an instant to realize that the Pharisee had worse things in mind for her than public humiliation. He wanted her stoned! She would have collapsed into a heap if he had not been holding her up roughly by the arm.

Mary wanted to search the young rabbi's eyes to see if they were kind, but did not have a chance. He seemed to be intent on making markings in the sand with a stick. *If I could only see his eyes! Then I would know if He would be condemning or not.*

The Pharisee and some others kept hurling accusations about her, but He did not respond. Curiosity began to nudge away the fear as she began to question why He was being so calm. Then He looked up, although his voice was quiet, it held so much authority that a thrill ran down her spine.

"Let him that is without sin cast the first stone!"

Mary waited for the sickening thud of that first stone to meet its mark and prayed that it would knock her out instantly. It did not come. It never came. She checked to see what he was writing on the ground, then she looked up at his face. It was kindly and full of tender forgiveness! Out of the corner of her eye, she saw the men slink away one by one, until even the haughty Hibernim was gone.

Now Yeshua's voice was soft and gentle, "Neither do I condemn you. Go, sin no more."

Although that was several weeks ago, it was etched in her mind
as clearly as if it had been yesterday. Since then, she has had no work
at all. She hunted all over town for a respectable job, but everyone
looked down on someone who had been a *zonah*. It made no difference
that she had not wanted to be one. It made no difference that she
had no choice; it was either that or beg. Who would toss coins to
a beautiful young *talitha*, one that was obviously in perfect health?

When she was not looking for work, Mary frequently
trudged behind the Rabboni, Yeshua, at a respectful distance.
I have a feeling that she esteemed Him very highly, but
did not feel worthy to be seen in His Shekinah.

One evening, that had all changed. She got out her alabaster box
of rich ointment and cradled it between her hands. It had taken
her a year of careful saving to purchase the rare perfume. She knew she
could sell it for a good price, to survive a little longer, but that is not
what she wanted to do with it.

"Yeshua," she whispered in her mind, as the tears slid down
her cheeks," *will you understand what I am trying to do?"*
As she plodded along the empty street, she had the alabaster ointment
carefully concealed within the folds of her garment. She had overheard
one of the Hibernim inviting Yeshua and His disciples for a meal and
was determined to offer this rebbe, this healer, this most wonderful
friend, her supreme gift in gratitude for what He had done for her.

In the distance, she saw the group of men strolling
toward their supper appointment.
Her heart squeezed with fear even while her feet took her
closer to the gleaming mansion. She saw the men disappear
one by one through the enormous doors. What if her enemy
was within those portals? She knew it was most probable.

The porter had left the door slightly ajar to let in the evening breezes. Mary slipped in and followed the sounds of the deep muted voices. They led her to men sitting on couches in a massive dining room.

Suddenly, she saw Him and she had eyes for Yeshua only. With a cry on her lips, she hurried over and sank to her knees. Yeshua," she whispered. "Yeshua, Yeshua!" *Oh that He will know how grateful I am for all He has done for me!*

As she opened the alabaster box for the first time, a sweet perfume wafted through the air. Someone sniffed depreciatingly, she heard a critical comment or two, but they barely registered.

"You saved my life, you saved my life," she breathed, as the tears of adoration and gratitude flowed down her cheeks and washed away the dust from His feet. With reverential tenderness, Mary lifted each one and dabbed at them with her flowing locks until no dust smudges remained. While she was massaging them with her fragrant oil, there was a lull in the conversation. Mary looked up.

Yeshua rested His hand lightly on her abundant tendrils and tilted her chin with one finger so that she would look directly at Him.

"Your sins are forgiven." His voice was deep rich, and oh so kindly.

She gazed rapturously into His eyes, He spoke again,

"Your faith has saved you go in peace."

Somehow, Mary found her way to the door, clutching the broken alabaster box to her bosom. She walked back to her house as if in a dream, knowing beyond the shadow of a doubt that she would follow Him wherever He went and serve Him with her whole heart.

DEAR DIARY,

For well over two years, Yeshua has been teaching and healing throughout Judea, I go with Him when I can. He greets His followers early in the morning, many of them are still with Him until evening, and often late at night. Even though His kindly face is often lined with weariness, He is always gentle and patient with the eager, although sometimes rude, crowds.

How can He bear having people jostle Him about constantly? I would be most uncomfortable.

I have been feeling so nervous lately, it is because there is an undercurrent of resistance stemming from the religious leaders. They seem intent on sowing discord among those that are seekers after righteousness. Wherever He goes, there are a few that are determined to heckle him. The strain is showing on Yeshua's dear face, I pray earnestly that His Father will protect Him. What else can a poor mother do for a well-known leader?

7th Cheshvan

October 23rd

DEAR DIARY,

Mary'am of Magdala, myself, Salome and a few others try to be of
service to Yeshua, I know we all yearn to do more. We are becoming
close, like sisters, because of our mutual concern for Yeshua's welfare.
Oh, *El' Elohim,* protect Your dearly beloved Son!

I believe He is quite aware of how often assassins are in the crowd. Spies
are also sent to trip Him up on His words. That is what puts the
strained look on His features, that and the constant giving of
Himself in heartfelt service to the poor and needy. Sometimes,
I wish He would flee like a bird to the mountains where there is
safety; but of course someone as noble as He would not consider
running away from His responsibilities! He will press onward toward
whatever goal the Father has planned for Him. I do not know how
this increasing animosity will end, and I dread finding out.

5th Adar

February 15th

DEAR DIARY,

I was looking forward to springtime and another season
of being with Yeshua on His missionary journeys,
but He told me it would not be safe.

It is so hard to stand back and just let things happen. What
could a helpless *aant'at* do to prevent the catastrophic
unfolding of events anyway? Many times a day, I pray with
groanings that cannot be expressed in words that Yahweh
will spare my Son. *Why do You not answer me?*

Oh, Yeshua, Yeshua, must You provoke the Hibernims so with Your
straight talk? Can't You flatter them like—oh, forgive me for writing
that. I know You would never stoop to something so base.
There are awful rumors circulating but I see so little of Him nowadays
that I cannot ascertain which are true, and which are not.
It frightens me to see such hatred in the eyes of the Sanhedrin.
I have seen the glint of a dagger more than
once in the hand of one whom
I am sure is a hired assassin.
I cannot sleep well at night for worrying about Yeshua and it
provokes the boys; they think I love Him more than them.

10th Nisan

April 2nd

DEAR DIARY,

We were in *Yerushalayim* like thousands of others because of the
Passover. One would think the walls would burst at the seams with so
much activity. The multitude went wild when they saw
Yeshua riding into the city on the foal of a donkey.
Why did I not find it stirring? My heart
clenched with fear. What's wrong with me that I am so
apprehensive these days? The crowd seemed convinced
that He was about to set up an earthly kingdom.

I happened to notice that our local small town baker was crowded
into a doorway directly across the narrow street from me.
He had a troubled look on his face,
but most everyone else went wild with excitement.

Even before Yeshua paused to weep over Yerushalayim,
I knew something was seriously wrong. I knew in my heart,
where keen perception grows,
that this display was like a mirage in the desert.

Why do I suspect that it will not last?
Oh, what anguish these misgivings are causing me.
I wish with all my heart that I could believe that the multitudes are
solidly behind him and that He will take the world by storm . . .
I must stop writing. These thoughts are causing
me such nervous tension!

29th Nisan

April 9th

DEAR DIARY,

All week long, there has been such tumult in the streets. Yeshua
advised me to stay where it is safe. There is always excitement when
pilgrims come from such faraway places to worship
in the Holy City; but there is an undercurrent of something
else this year, an attitude that feels dangerous.

I have been sitting on the rooftop of our host's house quite often,
anxiously watching the noisy throng. It is easy to pick out the richly
clothed Hibernim and Sadducees as well the heavily armored Roman
soldiers. It is easy to spot the beggars crouching against buildings, but
the rest are like an endless stream of color, mixing, separating, and then
flowing together once again. It is definitely safer not to be down there.

Oh *Yerushalayim*, beloved city,
what is going to happen to you? I remember the
day Yeshua wept over you and His prophetic words.

DEAR DIARY,

I am so distressed, there is something fearful in the air!
I can feel it. The animosity towards Yeshua
is as thick as an ominous cloud. I know the religious rulers are
planning evil against Him. I know He is not safe here.
Oh, Yeshua, Yeshua, I wish You hadn't come. I wish You would
hide, or, better yet, call down angels to protect You.
I wish that *HaShem* would help You to escape like He did when they
wanted to cast You off the embankment in Navara. I fear for You!
I'm so afraid that the Great I AM will not save you, not this time.

Oh, El'Elohim, have mercy, please, please
have mercy on my son.

DEAR DIARY,

Yeshua and His *talmidim* went to a friend's place to celebrate the Passover. I would have given all that I have to have been there with Him but I was not invited.

I've been spending much of my time on the rooftop, gazing at the darkening sky. I think I saw Him leave John Mark's house and head for the olive gardens. Oh, I wish, I long for Him to stay where it is safe . . . a little safer, at least.

A servant offered me some food, I cannot bear to think of eating right now.

Later, much later, I saw soldiers with torches heading towards the gardens.
It can mean no good. Oh, that my eyes could see in the dark and penetrate through trees so I could know what was going on. Someone tell me, please, what is that rabble rousing in the streets all about at this hour? What is going on? Tell me, please, tell me what is going on?

Oh, Yeshua, Yeshua, are you safe? Is it well with You?

Later...

DEAR DIARY,

A man is running down the street, I see him.
Would he be coming to this house? He runs like Yochanam.
He sees me and is calling my name. He wants me to come,
it must be something about Yeshua! I must go. Now !

2nd Iyyar

April 12th

DEAR DIARY,

They crucified my son today.
I can hardly bear to sit down and write,
yet if I do, perchance there will be healing for my spirit.
Nay, there cannot be healing. Nothing can heal my torn, bleeding,
broken spirit. There is no grief as insufferable as losing
a *tinoki* in such a cruel,
heartless way. I can not go on. The agony is too great to bear.

2nd Iyyar

April 12th

DEAR DIARY,

Sleep has fled, my head is pounding terribly,
so I might as well try to put my thoughts on paper.
It has always helped in the past. I shall
never be able to get those horrible scenes out of my mind.
No one can describe my suffering as I stood on the dark,
wind-swept hill watching
my son, my beautiful, dear, precious son writhe in pain
while the lightning flashed around Him.
The lightning seemed to be trying, but never quite succeeding,
to strike Him like vicious serpents.
Oh, why did they do this to Him? He was always so good,
so kind, and loving. Why did *HaShem* allow it?

There is one thin shaft of light that has pierced my agony.
Even while dear Yeshua hung there on the cross,
He remembered how much I would be
suffering, weakly calling out to me,
"Madam, behold Thy Son!"
My eyes were drawn to His, although I beheld much concern
for me in them, I also saw so much pain that I could
hardly handle it. They seemed to be saying, *I am doing
this for you,* Imma, *and all of mankind as well.*

His eyes turned toward Yochanam, He said to him,
"Behold your mother." I think He was asking His beloved
disciple, Yochanam, to care for me because His brothers
are still irritated or confused by the kind of man He is.
Yochanam has a tender heart, much like Yeshua's own.
In some way, in a soothing way, it will seem like
having Yeshua back home with me.

Yochanam will not be gone all the time doing miracles
and drawing crowds, like Yeshua did.

Oh, how could I forget even for a moment? He
won't be gone ...gone... like ...ohhhh...

Much later, I sank to my knees, sobbing my heart out.
Yochanam knelt beside me. He let me bury my head on his
shoulder, just like a *Chavivi* son would, while he wrapped his
tefilah shawl about me. Sadly, the comfort was meager.

DEAR DIARY,

My thoughts have turned to Yosef.
It seems so long ago since he passed, yet I still long for the
touch of his comforting arms around me at times. Nay,
not even Yosef could comfort me . . . not this time!

Another awful scene is burned on my mind. Even now, my
stomach heaves when I think of it. They thrust a spear into that
precious side, that dear, dear body that I have so lovingly bathed
and dressed time without number when He was a wee *tinoki*.
They so cruelly thrust a sharp vicious spear into His side!

Why did they do it? How could they do it? No one has ever been
more loving and thoughtful. No one, yet that is how He has been
repaid. Out gushed water and blood,. I thought my heart was
broken before, but it seemed to break anew when I saw that.
Oh, the agony He must have suffered.

I did not want to watch, but I could not help but see when they threw
Him down on the cross beam and drove those awful nails right into
his wrists. What a terrible sight! His face was etched with agony
but never, not once, did He lash out at those calloused soldiers.
I was standing there with my face buried in my hands much of
the time, yet the terrible scenes are burned into my memory.
They stood there mocking Him, not only the soldiers, but others as
well. Those that are supposed to be our religious leaders were the
worst! Wasn't it enough to see that He was going to die—
die the most shameful of all deaths? Could they not have
left Him alone—given Him some privacy, at least

But no, no, they had to hurl scathing mockery at Him.

It is permitted for women to give victims a sop drenched with vinegar and gall to ease the pain. I offered it to Him, but He weakly shook his head when He found out it was drugged.

I guess He wanted to endure all the suffering, but why? I must go. The household is beginning to stir and they will need something to eat.

DEAR DIARY,

There is nothing to write. Nay, that's not quite true. There are
things to write, but I am almost too heavy of heart to pick
up a reed pen and try to push it across the page.
I might as well record one thing while I am here.

We were able to care for His matchless body,
so bruised and torn now,
I helped wrap the cloths around Him for the burial.
It was the last tender act I could do for Him before He was buried.
He, who has always been so good to me!
I am glad we still had the myrrh that He was given as a babe. We
couldn't prepare His body properly because it was nearly evening,
our Shabbat would soon begin. On the first day of the week,
we will prepare ointments and spices to do what we can
to embalm Him since we were not allowed to do so sooner.

It grieves me to think that there will be no open *Shiva*, week of
mourning, for Yeshua. . We certainly would not be able to find ten men
brave enough to serve as *minyan*, not even among his own disciples.

Please. Please, do not let me think about where He is now!
If He was forsaken of *El' Elyon*, the Most High, as He cried
out, then there is only one other place for Him to be.

Surely, *Hades* would vomit out such a perfect man.

How can I go on? It felt like the sword had been plunged even deeper than ever into my heart when He cried out, *"Eloi, Eloi, lama sa-bach-tha-ni "* (My *El Elohim*, my *El Elohim*, why hast Thou forsaken Me?) The light of my life has been snuffed out. The light of the world has been snuffed out, the darkness not only surrounds me but it seems to have invaded my entire being. Why do I try to write? My life is so bleak. There is nothing to look forward to. If Yeshua is. was, not the Son of *El Elohim* then…I am lost, He is lost, and the WHOLE WORLD

IS LOST!

DEAR DIARY,

I must have sunk unto the floor in a dead faint because Yochanam
carried me to my private sleeping bench, placing a cover over me.
He slipped something between my lips, an herbal concoction perhaps,
and gave me a drink of water. I fell into a deep, heavy, dreamless,
but not restful, sleep. My head is still dull and aching.
In the gray light of a cool dawn, I am huddled over this tear-stained
parchment once again, like the friend I cling to it in my hour of need.

DEAR DIARY,

Yochanam laid his hand on my shoulder and asked me if I would care to share what I had been writing with him. I shrugged my shoulders slightly, he took that as an affirmative. I sat there leaning against his arm while he read. When he was done, he wrapped his arms around me, our tears mingled. I'm glad he is comfortable holding me close, now that Yeshua and Yosef are both gone. Under normal situations, a man is forbidden
to touch a woman unless she is his wife or child, so it is good that Yeshua told Yochanam to take care of me. Sometimes, a woman needs a man to hold her close and my own sons aren't up to it right now.

Eventually, our weeping lessened, after all, life must go on even though the light of our lives has gone out.

Yochanam told me that at the end, Yeshua had commended His spirit into the hands of His Heavenly Father. That is some consolation, I suppose, but did Yahweh accept Him?

Oh, such bitterness is seeping into my bones.
I cannot live this way, but I have no strength to fight against it.
One more memory is haunting me. I may as well write about
it even though it is so oppressive. When I saw what they had
put on His head, something fierce welled up within me.
It was a wreath of terrible thorns, so sharp that blood
was coursing in rivulets down His cheeks.

I wanted, oh, how I wanted to snatch it off and fling it aside.
They were scoffing at His sacred claims of being a King!
Years of conditioning to be

Marilyn Friesen

quietly submissive rooted me to the spot. I had lovingly washed and combed those locks, and now they were matted, blood-stained. I had soothed that pallid brow countless times, kissed Him to sleep. Why am I doing this to myself? Why must I dredge up all these awful events? I want to forget, to wrap myself in a mantle of pleasanter memories; the horror of what has happened tears at me.

Even the heavy temple veil was torn in half! I am so frightened. It seems like evil is stronger than good, where will it all end?

When I lay aside my writing instruments, I hope sleep will grip me once again. I am so terrified of the unknown while awake, I so rarely fall asleep, at least when I do there is oblivion for a short while.

Early tomorrow morning, some of His closest friends will accompany me to the tomb for our final acts of service to Him who we all loved so dearly. I know the *talmidim* will not go. They have lost all faith and hope. It has been a crushing disappointment for them, for all of us. But we must do this, and then somehow muddle blindly onward without the light of our lives present.

Yeshua, oh, Yeshua, do You know how much we are hurting?

4th Iyyar

April 14th

DEAR DIARY,

It is much later, now. It seems like this long night will never end, yet I dread seeing His precious face so still and cold in death. Will the agony ever lessen for me?

HE IS RISEN!!

DEAR DIARY,

Yeshua, how I adore you! How I marvel at how true
Your claims to be the Son of *El Elohim* and the Mashiach were.
Yehoshua! I cannot say Your Holy Name enough. Oh, the wonders of
beholding Your radiant face once again. Never has the healing of my
spirit been so rapid, so complete!

Tears of grief transformed into tears of rejoicing on this holy day.
Never in my wildest dreams had I expected to see Him alive, as the
resurrected Son of *El Elohim*, healed in body, radiant in spirit.

It has been a day of thrilling excitement and rejoicing. One
moment I flew into Yosef's arms sobbing with joy, "He lives,
He lives," while Yosef shouted in return, "I knew it, I knew
it, He *is* the Son of God, Hallelujah, He rose again!"
Never before Yosef's death had I seen my husband so exuberant
but now he couldn't get over the joy, the wonder
of Jesus coming to life again.
While we were rushing about telling everyone
who would listen that Jesus had returned,
Mimi joined us, then Grandpa, and loved ones
whom we had laid to rest some years before, each radiant
with joy, pulsating with vitality, bursting with news
of the great resurrection story.
So much pain was healed in an instant, and as I kissed Yeshua's
nail scarred hands my heart welled in worshipful adoration.

Later when our deceased loved ones once more faded from our sight, it wasn't with such deep sorrow. Death is not victorious! We will meet again because of Yeshua! I don't feel inclined to hire mourners ever again. Why should we? We'll live again!

Now, even more so than during His years as Rabban
and Healer I will gladly be in the background;
I want to mingle with the crowd
and just be another of His ardent followers.
I want to cling to His sacred feet, to be His bond servant.
Nothing could give me more pleasure than doing
His every bidding.
I now I can forever bask in His Shekinah in the form of the Holy Spirit.
Oh, I am so glad that He arose!

7th Tammuz

June 15th

Dear Diary,

Yeshua is gone again, but this time the departure
was much easier to bear. He has left to be with
His Heavenly Father, where He certainly
deserves to be yet His Comforting Presence will be
with each one of us who love and serve Him.
He is preparing a place for all of His *Chavivi*.
Thank you, thank you, oh, Heavenly Father for letting me
care for Him for just a little while during the time
He dwelt among us. Now I understand that the veil of the
temple was rent. It was to show us that we could reach
You directly after He died. Thank you for letting me
kiss those nail-wounded hands one last time.
He is whole once again, but those scars are left to remind
us of the tremendous cost of our redemption.

Taudi, for those final glorious moments on the hillside
while we watched Him ascend to Heaven.
I know that He must return to You from whence He came, but,
oh, I will cherish Your Shekinah which is with me daily.
One day, oh marvelous day, we will meet again!

With **A'Ahava**, (love,) and rejoicing, Mary'am

YESHUA

He was a man
Youthful loving strong
He did not seek the pain
The crush of thorns
On his noble, godly brow.

He was a Man
With mangled, whip-lashed back
The one whose soul is pure
Endured our lack
Our burdens, shame, and guilt.

He was a Man
The cup He did not spurn
Though mocked by maddened mobs
Broken, bleeding, torn
Hung on a cruel cross.

He is our God
Weighed down by all our sin
He carried so much blame
So we could reach his home
Forgiving through it all.

Oh Victory!
From a splendid throne He rules
With power to set men free
From Satan's bonds so cruel
The resurrected King!

GLOSSARY

Aant'at:: Women

Abba: Papa

Adonai: Lord of Lords. El Elohim is our Master, and we are His slaves, Therefore we must obey Him.

Ain Karim: Town where Zacharias and Elisabeth possibly lived

Akeret ha bay-it: women are the foundation of the home

alef bet: alphabet

Aleichem: : neighbors

Amen Alleluia': words of praise

Ayopokoitoo: Tomboy (Greek)

Banoah: Blessed

Beth Lechem: Bethlehem

Caleb Ben-Reuven:-Hana's betrothed

Huppah: wedding canopy

Chanukahs: Festival of lights

Chava: The Hebrew former of the name Eve

Chavivi: My beloved

Dohd: Uncle

Dohda: aunt

El'Elohim: El Elohim, the Creator

El Shaddai: Savior

Geshem: latter rain

HaShem: the Name: Used in reference to El Elohim

Hana, Dorcas, and Naomi Mary'am's sisters

Hibernim: religious ruling class, Pharisees

Imma: Mama

Kelev: dog

Ketubah: marriage contract

Khan: inn

Mashiach: Messiah

Matzo: crisp biscuit of unleavened bread eaten during Passover

Mitzvahs. ritual immersion symbolic of spiritual cleansing.

Nesher: bird of prey

Navara: Nazareth

Niphal", sorry, remorse

Mousht: a type of edible fish

Rabban: Rabbi. Literally Our Great One

Ruth and Lydia: Friends from Beth Lechem

Shabbat: Sabbath

Shekinah: His Glory, or the Presence of El Elohim

Sheol: Abode of the dead

Riba, yeled: both mean child

Talitha: girl

Taudi: Thank you

Tinoki: little child. It appears to be more a term of endearment.

Tefilah: prayer shawl

Tzedakah: deeds of kindness, justice

Torah: the law of El Elohim as revealed to Moshe

Wimple: Veil, or head, and neck covering

Yahweh: El Elohim

Yaakov: Jacob

Zaidi: grandfather

Yerushalayim: Jerusalem

Yeshua, Jesus,

Yeled: young child

Israelites: Yisraelites

Yerushalayim.: Jerusalem

Yosef and Mary'am: Joseph and Mary

Zonah: immoral woman, prostitute